Tender Fingerprints

A true story of loss and resolution

— Brad Stetson —

ZONDERVAN™

GRAND RAPIDS, MICHIGAN 49530 USA

Tender Fingerprints
Copyright © 1999 by Brad Stetson

Requests for information should be addressed to:

Zondervan, *Grand Rapids, Michigan 49530*

Library of Congress Cataloging-in-Publication Data

Stetson, Brad.
    Tender fingerprints: a true story of loss and resolution / Brad Stetson.
      p. cm.
    Includes bibliographical references.
    ISBN: 0-310-24309-2 (Softcover)
    1. Stillbirth—Religious aspects—Christianity. 2. Stetson, Brad.
3. Consolation. I. Title.
BV4907.S74 1999
248.8'66'092-dc21   99-27101
  [B]   CIP

This story is true. Quotations and remarks are adapted from actual conversations and statements. Some minor events and conversations have been fictionalized for the sake of narrative texture. Pseudonyms are often used to preserve people's privacy.

All Scripture quotations, unless otherwise indicated, are taken from the *Holy Bible: New International Version®*. NIV®. Copyright © 1973, 1978, 1984 by International Bible Society. Used by permission of Zondervan Publishing House. All rights reserved.

Interior design by Laura Klynstra

Printed in the United States of America

---

02 03 04 05 06 07 08 /❖ DC/ 10 9 8 7 6 5 4 3 2 1

Praise for Tender Fingerprints
by Brad Stetson

Tender Fingerprints is an honest and painful story which heals even as it brings tears to the eye. May God comfort many couples who have lost children through the words of this moving testimony.

There's little that can happen to us that is more difficult to deal with than the death of one of our children. It's all so wrong—so out of order. I've never read a more moving account of how one couple came to a point of personal resolution that not only lets us see and feel the imperfect struggle, but also lets us walk alongside of them through the ups and downs of their faith.

One of the most profound feelings following the loss of a child is that of being alone. Brad Stetson's generous, intimate account of his loss will help countless others move from this place of isolation and darkness to that better place of hope and light.

Brad Stetson faces unblinkingly his own weakness and sin, his anger with God, and his depression over the stillbirth of his son. His sometimes brutal honesty leads the reader to ponder God's ways and prepare for the suffering that will come to each of us eventually. For that reason, this is both a hopeful book—and a helpful one.

SUSAN OLASKY,
assistant editor, *World* magazine

This book portrays a frank, gripping account of what a young couple experienced with regard to a phenomenon that is virtually ignored in our society: the birth of a stillborn child. The author pulls no punches. He graphically reveals the pain and emotions he and his wife endured when their hopes and dreams crashed as they saw their beloved baby born, strangled to death by his own umbilical cord in his mother's womb. There is much to learn from this down-to-earth true story.

ALVIN J. SCHMIDT, PH.D.,
professor emeritus of sociology, Illinois College, Jacksonville, Illinois

Tender Fingerprints is a beautifully written and riveting story. But one warning: it is also a heart wrenchingly sad tale that clearly communicates the agony of losing a baby. In the end, though, Stetson's insightful narration shows us what it means to live with grief and to reach the "new normal." For people everywhere who have suffered miscarriage, stillbirth, or the loss of a newborn, here is a book that illustrates your grief, and points the way home.

JOSEPH G. CONTI, PH.D.

To my wife, Nina, a truly courageous woman

Contents

Acknowledgments

I offer my deepest thanks to those who, in various ways, contributed to the publication of this book. I am uniquely indebted to Joseph G. Conti, who patiently listened to me read him each chapter upon its completion. His reflections and suggestions were a great assistance.

Everyone at Zondervan has been extremely helpful, in particular, Diane Bloem, Joyce Ondersma, John Topliff, and Lori Walburg. My editor at Zondervan, Sandy Vander Zicht, has been wonderfully supportive, and her editorial ideas always sensitive and insightful.

My wife, Nina, contributed to this book in obvious ways, but also in subtle and indescribable ways. It is our story together, and it is her story alone. This will always be her book.

Brad Stetson
New Year's Day, 1999

A Word to the Reader

*A*s so many people find out, when a child is born to you, the world changes. Or, perhaps more accurately, you change, and change so profoundly that the ways in which you understand the world become significantly different. You awake from a slumber of sorts and begin to see the world as it truly is.

This book is about seeing the world as it truly is, in all of its painfulness, promise, and ambiguity. It's also about learning to trust God amidst life's greatest difficulties. I do not represent the experiences I will describe as definitive, my interpretation of those events as unquestionable, or the spiritual lessons I unfold as uncommonly insightful. I only wish to present honestly what happened to me, the mistakes I made in dealing with it, and what, through God's grace, I was able to learn from it all, for I believe that valuable lessons for others can be gleaned from my experience.

In some ways my story is rather like an explorer's tale, the recollections of one who traveled to a distant land, saw things he had never seen before, and then returned to his home to tell others about what he saw and learned.

If you are one of those who, like me, has traveled to that place of grief—which is at once distant yet close—and my reports do not match your own, that is understandable, as the set of experiences each of us brings to our individual voyages inevitably affects what we see and how we see it. So please hear what I have to say with an open mind and ears willing to hear, knowing that I offer it only as my own story and as a vehicle through which you might come to a deeper knowledge of Jesus Christ.

It may be that you are able to learn things from my story which I myself could not or would not. If so, I heartily salute you, since the ability to learn and grow from the suffering, turmoil, and mistakes of others is a great skill, and one of the keys to walking the path of wisdom to which God calls us. "Wisdom is supreme; therefore get wisdom. Though it cost you all you have, get understanding" (Proverbs 4:7).

I humbly invite you then to look with me now at a part of my life and see how it might strengthen and enrich your own.

*W*e must not wallow in our memories or surrender to them, just as we don't gaze all the time at a valuable present. But get it out from time to time, and for the rest hide it away as a treasure we know is there all the time. Treated this way, the past can give us lasting joy and inspiration.

Dietrich Bonhoeffer

Chapter 1

A Perfect Beginning

I never really liked children. In fact, when I was a kid, I was something of a bully. I delighted in seeking out those smaller than me and picking on them. Since I was always bigger and stronger and faster than most of the other kids around me, it was a risk-free venture.

There was one young boy in particular to whom I remember being especially unkind. His name was Todd Lewis, and he was in my seventh grade gym class. He had profoundly large front teeth, leading everyone to call him, with the malevolent glee unique to junior high boys, "Horse-face." I spent an entire school year wondering aloud, to the amusement of the other boys and to the humiliation of Todd, how his teeth had grown to their gargantuan size. Did he chew on trees? Did he build dams? Was he part of a fluoride experiment gone terribly wrong?

Through it all, this young boy seemed to remain remarkably good-natured and friendly. At the end of the year he wrote in my yearbook, with the simple honesty and humility of a pure heart, "Brad, you always made fun of me, and I wanted to make fun of you, but I could never find anything to tease you about. Have a good summer. Todd."

He moved away the next year, but I never forgot his good nature and precocious equanimity. I wonder now if he only suffered in silence, if the pain we caused him was too much for him to openly express.

As I became an older teen and young adult my mean streak mellowed. I came to Christ as a high school senior, became a little more secure as a person, and more mature as a young man. Still, though, I did not have any special affection for children and never envisioned myself becoming a father. In fact, from the time I married at age twenty-four until my wife Nina and I decided to try to start a family some four years later, I had no parental impulse I could feel, no burning desire to assume that ultimate human responsibility.

My wife, though, certainly yearned to be a mother. She had always, as a girl and young woman, been deeply interested in kids. Playing mommy, baby-sitting, helping care for neighbors' children—she always had a deep and strongly felt maternal sense. Even in high school, when I met her, she would frequently talk about children. As she moved into adulthood she became a preschool teacher and then a kindergarten teacher, learning and preparing in many ways for the time when she would have a child of her own.

I can remember quite clearly when I became interested in having children. Oddly enough, my paternal feelings grew out of a sense of obligation. My parents had no grandchildren, and I simply felt obliged to change that. My two older brothers, who both had been married longer than I, were each childless, with apparently no plans to change the situation. As my parents' friends became grandparents, I began to feel a sense of having failed them, even betrayed them. I knew that having children to please parents was certainly not the script for adults in the 1990s—and maybe not a very wise course at any time—but I felt a relentless sense of duty that I could not shake. And I saw that Nina was ready. Now nearly thirty, she was itching for motherhood. Baby magazines started showing up on the coffee table, television shows about having babies were always on, and she began asking me which baby names I liked. Her biological clock was sounding off, and this most powerful yearning of the female heart was etched in her face.

So, at perhaps an inopportune time for me—I was in graduate school, earning a thousand dollars a month as a teaching assistant—Nina and I decided to start a family. We had it all figured out: we'd have two or three kids, two years apart, they'd be beautiful, precocious, and always well-behaved. We were so confident that everything would go according to our plan, we didn't even consult God about it. His will? Of course it matched are own; after all, we really wanted to have children.

The peaking of the desire for kids is something that always changes one's life. It does so if you succeed in having a baby; it does so if you are never able. There was no way I could have known, though, that hot July in southern California in 1990, that the events which were in store for Nina and me would be so profoundly powerful and trans-formative—and so totally unexpected.

Conceiving a child was, for us, fairly easy. After having been off the birth-control pill for three months—in order to avoid the risk of birth defects it might cause—we began try-ing to get pregnant that summer and succeeded in December.

This was somewhat remarkable since Nina had always ovulated irregularly. She had the "cycle from hell," as she used to call it, because one month she would ovulate at twenty days, the next at thirty-six days, the next at twenty-five. She never knew when she'd be fertile, and so while we were trying to conceive, we had to make love constantly. This might not seem so bad, but even sexual intimacy can become burdensome if it has to be done by the clock and calendar, whether you're in the mood or not.

I remember while I was watching a college football game one fall Saturday afternoon, she called me upstairs and purred, "I think I'm ovulating now, honey, won't you do it to me?"

I told her to wait until halftime.

I returned as soon as the marching bands took over the field, and Nina was in quite a tiff. After I apologized and spent fifteen minutes trying to calm her down, we got on with it. But there was a clock in my head ticking down the start of the third quarter, and I was disinterested. When she complained about it, I yelled at her. She quickly got out of bed, declaring, "That's no way to have a baby!"

The stress of having to manage our intimacy according to her ovulatory cycle was becoming apparent, and had we not conceived after a few months, it certainly would have become a significant source of friction for us.

I deliberately use the plural to describe our pregnancy, since I understood at the time, quite clearly, that I would become pregnant too.

I understood that the child inside my wife would be mine, just as he would be hers. He would be ours, not only in the technical biological sense but also in the emotional and spiritual sense. He would be a sacred trust from God, and his life would partake of my life. I would be his father, the one who would give birth to him, not physically, but psychologically and morally. I would be charged with forming his manhood, with showing him what it means both to respect others and to win respect. It would be my responsibility to lay upon him the behavioral expectations that would be both his burden and blessing. I would also communicate to him through word and deed the love of Jesus Christ for him, and the promise of the Gospel, and the meaning of Christian commitment.

I did not think that it would be my role to lavish upon him unconditional love—except for in his early years. His mother, I assumed, would always be there to do that. I thought it would be best for him if, as he grew, he knew my love for him was related in an important way to the quality of his conduct. It would be best for my boy to know that his father desperately wanted him to be morally decent and humane, that I yearned so powerfully for him to love and honor God in his life, that how he treated other people would meaningfully affect how I felt toward him.

That may sound severe, and I wonder if I could actually hold to such high principle, but my sense of mission and obligation toward my son helped me, prenatally, to form a bond with him.

Indeed, from the moment I found out of his existence, I felt attached to him. I remember it clearly: I was lying in the bed one lazy Saturday morning just after Christmas, and my wife ran out from the bathroom frantically waving a home pregnancy test, shouting as though she had won a lottery, "I'm pregnant! I'm pregnant!"

I greeted these headlines with a feigned indifference, as I rolled over onto my stomach and grunted a sarcastic, "Great."

She skipped down the hallway like a schoolgirl who had just gotten an "A" on the final exam. She picked up the phone, and a minute later I could hear her chattering excitedly in Spanish to her Mexican mother. She was talking so fast it sounded like she was on fast-forward.

I breathed a prayer of thanks and thought about what I would say to my mother. How would I bring her and my dad the news of their first grandchild? I decided I would tell them straight out, since every time I called and said "Guess what?" they always became annoyed, fearing some tragedy or terrible event.

When I did call my parents later that week, after Nina had gone to her doctor and confirmed that she was pregnant, I followed my plan and gave them the news as soon as they picked up the phone.

"Well," I said a little nervously, "I'm just calling to tell you that Nina is pregnant."

"Oh, honey!" my mom gasped.

"Are you sure?" my dad asked.

"We're sure. We just went to Nina's doctor today and confirmed it," I said, anticipating my father's next question. Of course they were both happy, but they were restrained in their reaction, I suppose simply because they didn't know how to act at such tremendous news, and also because they feared that if they showed too much relief or joy I might take it as an insult. As if, "Well, it's about time!"

But they were undeniably happy and relieved at the news, and I felt tremendous satisfaction at being able to announce it to them. In fact, I felt proud at delivering to them a grandchild when my two older brothers, who had always outshone me in almost every way, had not. This was of course a perverse pride, but I found myself wanting to take responsibility for this new reality, as though somehow I had orchestrated it all.

From the day I knew Nina was pregnant, I noticed that in subtle ways I began to treat her differently and to think of her in a different way. I stopped thinking of her only as my wife, the woman to whom I was married, the person I lived with and with whom I spent most of my time. Now she became someone different, someone endowed by God with the mystical ability to carry life and give birth, someone who was a mother. And not only that, but the mother to my son, my offspring, my hope, and my heritage. She was a unique and special creation of God, whom I was called to love and cherish. Of course, she had always been that and always would be whether she had become pregnant or not, but I came to understand that more fully after she conceived.

And so, in my zeal to protect my baby and my wife, I took a new and sometimes strangely intense interest in her activities. For Nina there would be no alcohol; no coffee, too much caffeine; no Pepsi, too much caffeine; no jogging with Javert (our basset hound) on walks, too jarring for the baby; no sleeping on your stomach, too much pressure on the baby; no yelling or laughing too hard, bad for the baby; no bending over to pull weeds, bad for your back and the baby; no lifting of heavy objects, bad for your back and too much strain on your stomach, which is bad for the baby.

I was making it all up as I went along. Much of it was nonsense—except for the prohibition on alcohol and the limit on caffeine—but it made me feel like I was managing things. By issuing these decrees, I created the illusion in my mind that I was controlling the situation, that I was insuring a safe and healthy baby and mother, and that I was fulfilling all of my responsibilities and duties as a husband and father.

Of course my wife quickly tired of these bizarre declarations and ignored most of them. This led to innumerable arguments, all of which followed the same pattern.

"Honey," I would say with the certainty of a medical school professor, "you do realize that by running with the dog you are hurting our baby, don't you?"

"It does not."

"Oh, yes, it does, it does, don't do it. I don't want you to do it. Okay?"

"You're nuts," Nina would calmly say.

"Honey, I don't want you to run with Javert. You mustn't do that."

"It doesn't hurt anything!"

"Nina, don't yell! Do not yell!"

"Leave me alone."

"Promise me you won't yell," I would continue. "Promise me you won't yell."

Silence from her.

"Honey, promise me you won't yell at me. It's not good for baby Stetson. You've got to think about that."

These inane, childish exchanges usually lasted about fifteen minutes, sometimes more. Back and forth, back and forth. They were a tremendous waste of time. Invariably I would extract from her the promise I wanted, calling on her to forsake whatever particular forbidden activity it was she was engaged in at the time.

"Okay, I won't do it. I promise not to do it," she would say mechanically.

A few minutes later she would break her *faux* vow, and we would begin the game all over again. I don't know how we got anything else done.

But I could not control myself; it was a compulsion. I literally could not resist micromanaging her life. Partly it was the illusion of control over the health of my baby that drove me on and partly the feeling of self-satisfaction it gave me. I was in control, everything was on track, all systems were go, all lights were green, everything was okay, everything was going to turn out okay. Taking the time to express trust in God and to cultivate a dependence on him had not occurred to me.

But despite my consummately annoying behavior of heckling Nina, she fared well, and so did our baby. In fact, not one time did she become sick. She had no morning sickness at all, no spotting, not even the flu that winter. As a kindergarten teacher, she inevitably brought home the occasional cold or sore throat, but there was never anything more severe than that. A textbook-perfect pregnancy.

Her obstetrician, Dr. Steven Bowers, was a reassuring, eminently responsible doctor. The first time we saw him was when Nina was eight weeks pregnant. She had been given her pregnancy test in the office of her gynecologist, an elderly man who had abandoned obstetrics. The stress of being on call, working odd hours, fretting medical details, and paying exorbitant malpractice premiums had driven him out of the baby business. So when a patient of his became pregnant, he sent her to Dr. Bowers, a latter-day Marcus Welby. He was youthful, tall, and thin, with plain black-rimmed glasses and the demeanor and appearance of a young minister or kindly police officer.

When we first met him we sat in his humble little office in an aging medical building across the street from the hospital where we would have our baby. He was surrounded by pictures of his four young children and his wife, a young Mary Tyler Moore updated for the early 1990s. How could he have gone to medical school and had so many kids and still be no more than thirty-two or thirty-three years old?

He was reassuring and straightforward with us, giving us a schedule of prenatal appointments and tests, explaining everything he would be checking for along the way. Nina and I left his office feeling utterly secure and confident. Dr. Bowers exuded competence, and there was no question in our minds we were in good hands.

The next time we saw him was when Nina was twelve weeks pregnant. After a little small talk he squirted KY jelly all over her slightly paunched stomach and pressed his Doppler microphone to it, and, as if on cue, we could hear our baby's heartbeat for the first time.

It was breath-stopping. *Pum-pum, pum-pum, pum-pum* it went rapidly, accompanied by the background swishing and thumping noises of Nina's body.

"Sounds like a boy," Bowers said, with a hint of a smile.

"You're kidding, right?" I said quickly.

He chuckled, and Nina said, embarrassed, "Yes, Brad, he's kidding."

To hear our baby's heartbeat was at once exhilarating and disconcerting to me. It was thrilling proof of another being, of our child's actual existence and independence. The life of our son had begun. But at the same time the sound incited apprehension in me. That lone heartbeat seemed a thin thread on which to hang my hopes and dreams. Could that single, solitary sound be enough to bring a whole baby through forty weeks and the trauma of birth? Never having been able to accept good news without imagining bad news, I grew nervous at the sound of my son's heartbeat. I felt the daunting responsibility to nurture his heartbeat and his little body into a full-term baby. A hard task on every count, especially since he wasn't inside of me.

When Nina was eighteen weeks pregnant, we had an ultrasound exam to check all of our baby's organs. We had the exam in a dark, quiet room, a setting befitting a solemn introduction. There we saw our baby for the first time.

The ultrasound technician moved methodically around the body, literally showing us all of our baby. At eighteen weeks he was fully developed; all of his organs were formed and in place. All that was left was for him to grow large enough to sustain himself. During the exam we saw the different lobes of his brain, the four chambers of his heart, his liver, his kidneys, his pancreas, his legs, hands, feet, fingers, and toes. We also saw that he was a boy.

"Buy blue," the technician said.

All the pieces of his life were there before us, in rich and surprisingly clear detail. We could even clearly see the profile of his nose, chin, and forehead.

"He looks like you," Nina said, at the same moment I said, "He looks like me."

Yes, he was my son all right; that much was clear even at eighteen weeks.

The technician froze the image on the screen and packed up her things as Nina and I held hands and gently kissed in front of the picture of our son. Even though the ultrasound exam was over, Nina and I gazed at the monitor for a few more minutes in a hushed and almost reverential silence. We understood the awesome value of this life God had given us. I squeezed Nina's hand tightly as we both sighed in amazement. Our baby looked serenely comfortable lying inside his mother, calmly sucking his thumb.

The technician gave us an ultrasound photo to take home. I propped it up on our kitchen counter and proudly displayed it to anyone who came into the house. That single picture meant so much to Nina and me. It was not only a picture of our son soon to come to us, but in my mind that little flimsy photo was also a token of our love. It represented the best thing we had ever done, the ultimate manifestation of our love and commitment as husband and wife, and the sacred trust of the Lifegiver himself.

To me the photo was also something of a trophy, a signifier of my virility and masculinity. It was as though it said, "Yes, I have done this, look what a big man I am." I was intensely proud of my boy and wanted to show him off, even in the form of a small, simple prenatal photo at eighteen weeks.

CHAPTER 2

Being Pregnant

*D*r. Bowers assured us he would call in a few days, after he received the radiologist's report on our ultrasound exam, to let us know how the baby's organs looked. He did as he promised he would.

"Everything's perfect," he immediately said as soon as I picked up the phone, sparing me any suspense.

"Are you sure, how about the heart?" I asked, as though I knew about some horrible defect.

"It's fine, everything's perfect," he answered, sounding a little confused. "You're going to have a healthy little boy. I wish I was going to be there to see it."

"What?"

"Well, I'm sorry to say we're moving back East. I've been offered a position with a large gynecological practice in Boston, and I'm going to have to take it. I'm sorry about that."

"Well, I'm sorry too," I said. "Nina's due in only a few months."

"But the good news is you are going to be in excellent hands," Bowers said. "Dr. Charles Lloyd is going to be taking over my patients. He's an excellent obstetrician; all the ladies really like him, and I'm sure things will go well for you."

Bowers was speaking at a faster pace. *This guy sure wants to get off the phone,* I thought.

Suddenly, he said, "Well, good luck to you. Bye now."

Before I knew it, and before I could say anything more, I was listening to a dial tone. Like contraband in the night, we'd been passed off to the unknown Dr. Lloyd.

Dr. Bowers of course had every right to move away and to do what he thought was in his family's best interests. But having him leave so abruptly, with no warning, made Nina and I feel cheated. Had we known earlier in the pregnancy that Dr. Bowers was considering leaving town, we might have sought out another obstetrician. We might have shopped around, interviewed them, researched them, and decided on our own whom to see. But now we had been assigned someone we did not know.

Of course we still could have found a new obstetrician on our own. But at this point, about halfway through the pregnancy, we were reluctant to go back to square one. We had grown attached to Dr. Bowers, trusted him completely, and were in some sense depending on him to help us physically and psychologically through the climax of this first pregnancy. But in the space of a few rushed seconds on the phone, that relationship came to a curt end.

A week later someone from Dr. Lloyd's office called and left a message on our answering machine.

"Hi, this is Christine from Dr. Lloyd's office," the perky voice piped. "I'm just calling to let you guys know you're due for your twenty-two week appointment in a couple weeks, so give us a call to set up a time. Thanks!"

She sounds like a cheerleader, I thought.

When we went to Dr. Lloyd's office for the first time, we were greeted by the happy Christine, who told us, "Have a seat, okay you guys?"

The office had a rock-and-roll atmosphere to it, with unusually loud pop music playing and magazines like *GQ, Rolling Stone, Elle, Cosmopolitan,* and *Self* laid out on the coffee tables, along with the doctor-office standards *People, Time,* and *Newsweek.* When it came time to see the doctor, we were ushered into Dr. Lloyd's office rather than an exam room.

His office was simple but hip, a lot of black and gray, with framed splashes of color on the walls. Dr. Lloyd himself was young, well-dressed, and very handsome, the dream of every mother for her daughter. Adorning a table next to his austere desk were pictures of himself in various settings: Dr. Lloyd at a restaurant with other very young and very good-looking people; Dr. Lloyd skiing down a mountainside; Dr. Lloyd receiving a diploma; Dr. Lloyd with his smiling parents.

Throughout our appointment Dr. Lloyd was extremely kind and patient with us, explaining what would happen the next four months or so. He was self-confident and quiet, obviously wanting to help us, and he set us at ease. I glanced at the diplomas hanging on the wall: B.S. in biology from UCLA, M.D. from University of San Francisco Medical School, residency in obstetrics and gynecology from USC.

Wow, I thought, *this guy is utterly competent. A man with this kind of training, just starting out his practice, is going to be very careful and thorough. We are in very good hands.*

After the exam we left the office, and as we were walking down the long hallway to the elevator, I asked Nina how she liked him.

"He's very nice," she said.

She sounded somewhat distant and stilted.

"Are you sure you like him?"

"Yes, I do, he's just fine," she said, sounding a little more earnest.

"Well, we can go and get ourselves another doctor if you want to, honey," I said, trying to make her feel free to ask.

"Look," she said firmly, "he's a good doctor. Dr. Bowers wouldn't have referred us to him if he wasn't. He'll do just fine."

That was enough for me, and I felt content. If she liked him enough to continue with him, then we would stick with him. I think the slight unease we felt was the residual effect of our commitment and attachment to Dr. Bowers. The MTV atmosphere of Dr. Lloyd's office didn't help either.

When we got home that day Nina spent hours decorating the baby's room. He wasn't due for months, but characteristically, Nina had taken care of everything well in advance.

The room was simple—white walls, with puffy little light blue clouds all around. And on the ceiling was a smiling yellow sun with what looked like some cows dancing around it. The crib and bassinet were in there and ready for action. On a small table off in one corner of the room sat a simple brown teddy bear, his black marble eyes large and clear. He looked almost happy as the light glinted off his eyes, giving them a momentary twinkle.

On the wall hung a small framed cloth on which were stitched the letters *BJ*. Nina's mom had made it a few weeks earlier when she found out that we were naming our baby Bradley John, after my dad (John) and me. The letters were simple but clear, their strong navy blue color standing out against the plain white background. *That will make a nice memento to give BJ when he's older,* I thought. He could always keep it in his room, reminding him, however faintly, of the love and nurture showered upon him from even before his birth.

Several weeks later we set off for our first Lamaze class. We were excited about it, because it meant the end was near. We showed up at the first class looking nervous and eager, just like the dozen or so other young couples there.

The class began with a funny and entertaining lecture from the teacher, a grandmotherly looking woman named Tedi, who regaled us with tales of the follies and foibles of childbirth: the man who was so intent on getting to the hospital quickly after his wife's water broke, that while she was in the living room waiting for him to help her out to the car, he sped off to the hospital, not realizing he was alone in the car until he pulled into the hospital parking lot; the woman who chose to forego an epidural or drugs of any sort so she could experience natural childbirth, only to regret it late in labor, to the embarrassment of her husband, whom she loudly berated with profanities for "doing this to me"; the man who was so attached to his softball team—and so unhappy that his wife "chose" a game day on which to have their baby—that he wore his team uniform and cleats to the hospital, so that he could leave immediately after the blessed event and catch the end of his game.

Everyone chuckled at the stories and said to their spouses, "You better not do that to me." Then it was more talking and an instructional movie. When it was over, I don't think we had learned much, but it was nonetheless a good experience for us. It communicated to us in an unmistakable way that we were not the first people in history to have a baby. Other people had gone through it too.

The next several weeks were uneventful. Nina was fine, the baby was fine, and I was nervous. But that is how things had been throughout the pregnancy, and we had grown accustomed to the rhythms and routines of being parents-in-waiting.

Around the time Nina was thirty weeks pregnant, we began going to see Dr. Lloyd every two weeks. The appointments were all the same: Christine was peppy and cheerful; Arlene, Dr. Lloyd's medical assistant, was quiet and businesslike; and Dr. Lloyd was impeccably dressed and completely self-confident. I would ask all sorts of questions about how long he would let Nina go in labor before he would call for a cesarean section, how we would know it was time to go to the hospital to have the baby, how long Nina would stay in the hospital, and so on.

"I don't think you're going to have any problems," he would always say to me. "Try to relax. Have a beer or something."

As the weeks wore on, I was getting more and more uncomfortable—and I wasn't even carrying the baby. Nina was the one who should have been uncomfortable, but she seemed hardly disturbed at all. She almost never complained. Her stomach had grown large but not extremely so. She carried BJ out in front of her, more so than off to the sides. She was small anyway, just five feet tall and ninety pounds, so every little bit would have showed, but her stomach never got very big.

Soon we started seeing Dr. Lloyd every week.

"You should do kick counts every hour," he told her when we saw him at thirty-six weeks. "You should be able to count at least ten kicks each hour, and if you don't, please call me."

Nina did her kick counts faithfully, often counting aloud, or having me sit next to her and count with her. Sometimes I did the counting for her because BJ's kicks were so strong that I could see him punching Nina from the inside. What must have been little hands or feet would pop up against her stomach, and it was easy to keep tabs on him. During the day he often slept, and so it became harder for Nina to keep count of his movement. She was still working as a kindergarten teacher—her school was in session year round, so she was working even though it was now August—thus her own activity further divided her attention. But she still made all her kick counts, and BJ's movements were strong.

Soon, it was time for Nina's thirty-eight week appointment. We were excited because we knew this meant the time was near. In fact, she could deliver at any time; she was already considered full term. Dr. Lloyd had told us that at this appointment he would check to see if her cervix was dilated at all, and go over with us again what to do when her water broke, what to expect in the hospital, and other details. It was a hot Friday afternoon, August 9, and when we got to Dr. Lloyd's office, the place seemed unusually busy.

Pregnant women came and went, looking very uncomfortable with their swollen bellies and penguin waddles. The phone rang constantly, and it seemed oppressively hot in the office, like the air-conditioning had broken. It was so unpleasant that even Christine's perennially perky voice was sounding soggy. After we waited in the hip office for a few minutes, Christine leaned out over the front desk and said to us, with her perkiness restored, "I'm sorry, you guys, but Dr. Lloyd was just called into the hospital to deliver a baby, so he needs to reschedule with you."

Of course Dr. Lloyd had a good excuse. Nevertheless I was distressed at not getting to see him, with Nina being at thirty-eight weeks. My irritation must have shown, because Christine said, "Don't worry, when it's your turn, he'll drop everything for you guys too, okay?"

"No problem," I said. "Can we see him tomorrow?" I knew that Dr. Lloyd saw patients on Saturday mornings.

"He's all booked for tomorrow. Sorry."

"Well, how about Monday, then?"

"Monday is Dr. Lloyd's day off. He usually water skis," Christine said, with inexplicable glee. "But how about Tuesday at 3:30, that would be great."

I didn't think it was so great, having one of Nina's final prenatal exams being delayed four days when she was thirty-eight weeks pregnant, but that was the earliest our doctor was available.

"Well, all right," I said. "We'll be back Tuesday afternoon."

"Have a great weekend, okay, you guys?" Christine chirped.

"Yeh, right," Nina said sarcastically as she propelled her swollen body forward with little steps.

The weekend was particularly uncomfortable, with Nina doing a lot of sitting while I walked around the house doing nothing in particular. When the new week began, I was relieved. We would be seeing Dr. Lloyd on Tuesday, and then we would have BJ shortly after that. What a relief it will be, I thought, to finally see BJ clearly, after waiting so many months, after fretting so many details, after envisioning so many horrifying scenarios.

What would it really be like to have a baby? The Lamaze classes we had been going to had given us some indication, but all of those movies looked sterile and clinical, the participants so perfect. I expected to see screaming women, fainting husbands, and frantic nurses. Was everybody really that calm? Would it really be the life-changing event people said it was? How would I react, how would Nina react, when we saw our precious baby emerge out of her and into the life we would all share?

As I went to bed that Sunday night, with Nina and BJ inside her lying peacefully next to me, I was in a very positive frame of mind. *Everything's going to be just fine,* I thought. I knew God loved us and was caring for us. First Peter 5:7 ran through my mind: "Cast all your anxiety on him because he cares for you."

My mind flashed back to several months earlier. My parents were visiting us, and my mom had accompanied me and the newly pregnant Nina while we walked Javert. During the walk Nina had playfully jumped up to grab a deflated white balloon that had somehow become stuck on a tree branch. As she pulled down the shriveled and lifeless balloon, I did one of my "Don't do that, you'll hurt the baby" speeches. But my mom cut me off, saying, "Come on, don't be ridiculous. It's going to be fine. Not everything ends in death, you know. Why don't you just lighten up?" As I remembered the incident, I thought she was right. I had no reason to expect disaster; everything was going to be perfectly all right. Why wouldn't it be?

The next night, Monday, August 12, Nina was lying on the couch watching television, and I was out walking Javert. Before she became pregnant Nina used to do all the walking of the dog, but after she had been pregnant for six months she had finally had enough of my transformation into something of an FBI agent monitoring her activities, and she insisted I start walking the dog. I had complained once too often about how jogging with the dog—or stepping off of curbs with him, or almost everything else—was bad for Nina and the baby. She had laid down the law: for the rest of the pregnancy either I walk Javert, or he wouldn't get a walk.

Taking the dog for walks was actually peaceful and stress-relieving for me. But because he walked at such an excruciatingly slow pace—until he caught a scent, and then he would start his awkward lope, occasionally tripping on his massive ears—it usually took a full hour. That night, when I returned from the walk, I opened the front door and saw Nina on the couch.

I said to her in a loud voice, "Hello, BJ, Daddy's home!"

"Wow, what a kick!" Nina said. "When he heard your voice just now he gave me the biggest kick I've ever felt. That was incredible. Maybe he's going to be a soccer player. Come over here, honey, and feel him."

I quickly walked over the to the couch and sat next to Nina and put my hand on her stomach where she said she felt the kick. He was still.

"Come on, BJ, kick again for Daddy. Come on, Daddy wants to feel you," I implored as I rubbed her stomach, a stroke which usually elicited another kick. But there was no movement.

"He must have exhausted himself with that monster kick," Nina said. "He's being quiet now."

I sat next to her for a moment more, waiting to feel movement, but none came, so I got up and went upstairs.

Later that night I came downstairs to check on Nina. She was sleeping angelically on the couch. Her left hand was at her side, and her right hand was resting tenderly on her rounded stomach. As I gazed at her, I thought about what a perfect mother she was, and what a great job she would do with BJ.

I also realized how incredibly fortunate I was. I had a sweet wife, and I was about to witness the long-anticipated birth of my first son. As I walked over to Nina to wake her and help her up the stairs to bed, I breathed a prayer of thanks to God for all of the joy in my life. I thought of King David, who, after he became king and heard God's promises to him through Nathan the prophet, said a prayer of gratitude which began with a recognition of his own undeservingness: "Who am I, O Sovereign LORD, and what is my family, that you have brought me this far?" (2 Samuel 7:18).

CHAPTER 3

"Oh God, Why?"

The next day, Tuesday, was blistering hot. I thought about how miserable Nina would be at her non-air-conditioned school, with all of the kindergartners panting and squirming. This was to be her last week of work before taking off to have the baby, however, so she wanted to hang in there, even though being nearly nine months pregnant in those conditions was a torment.

Our appointment to see Dr. Lloyd was at 3:30 that day, so at 3:00 I pulled into the driveway of Nina's school to pick her up. She came bounding out of the office with a slight grin, fanning herself with the few papers she was holding in her hand.

"Why must it be so hot?" she said quickly as she plumped her puffy body into the front seat and exhaled loudly. Her curly black hair was matted around her neck from perspiration.

"Honey, you look like Javert after a bath," I said, rubbing her sweaty neck.

"Thanks a lot. Just get us to Dr. Lloyd's office fast; they have good air-conditioning."

I sped away, and fifteen minutes later we were there.

As soon as we stepped out of the elevator and into the long hallway that led to Dr. Lloyd's office, we felt much cooler.

"Man, this building has air," I said.

We were silent the rest of the walk down the straight, empty corridor.

We entered Dr. Lloyd's office to the exclamation of Christine. "Oh, hi, you guys! Happy Tuesday!"

We replied "Hi" in unison, once again not matching her enthusiasm. We were alone in the waiting room, and after a short wait the quiet Arlene showed us back to the exam room. Nina left to give a urine sample, and Arlene and I remained behind, in a mildly awkward silence.

"It's almost time," she said, with her back to me as she reshuffled the magazines on the counter. I didn't realize she was talking about BJ, so I paused, leading her to turn around and say a bit more slowly, "Are you ready for the baby?"

"Oh, yes, we're ready to get it over with," I said, nodding. "Nina especially."

Nina then walked in. She made small talk with Arlene as she changed into a paper exam gown. Arlene took her blood pressure and weighed her.

"Well, you're perfect at 120," Arlene said as Nina got off the scale.

"I don't feel very perfect."

"Well, I wish I could weigh 120. I haven't weighed that much since high school."

Arlene left just as Dr. Lloyd walked through the door. He was dressed flawlessly once again. His starched white lab-coat stood out against his dark blue shirt and tie.

"You're almost there," he said, gently touching Nina on the shoulder. "It won't be long now. Let me just get a heart-beat from the baby, then I'll remind you about going to the hospital and checking in after your water breaks."

I was sitting down on a chair in the corner of the office. Nina lay back on the exam table as Dr. Lloyd pushed her flimsy gown up, squirted KY Jelly all over her belly, and rubbed it around.

"That stuff is always so cold," Nina said.

Dr. Lloyd picked up his Doppler microphone from the counter. "Okay," he said as he placed the small device on the middle of Nina's abdomen.

We could hear swishing and swashing as Nina's blood and body made noises the Doppler amplified. About a minute passed without Dr. Lloyd saying anything. This was not unusual; it had often taken about a minute to find the baby's heartbeat.

But after another minute passed, Dr. Lloyd shifted his weight from one foot to the other, and said with a slight sigh, "Okay, come on now."

I had been sitting with my head down, staring at the floor during this time, but now I looked up at Dr. Lloyd, and I noticed a look on his face I had never seen before. It was a combination of confusion and concern.

I quickly looked out the window into the bright daylight. My heart sunk into my stomach as I realized Dr. Lloyd was genuinely worried. I began to feel a strange tightness and nausea in my stomach, as a wave of sheer panic washed over me. I suppressed it, repeating silently to myself that everything was going to be okay. My heart began beating very rapidly. I cleared my throat. I shifted in my seat so I could see Nina. She was staring at the ceiling, expressionless, blinking her eyes rapidly.

"Is there a problem?" Nina asked with a slight quiver to her voice.

I looked at Dr. Lloyd for his response, but he was silent. He continued moving the Doppler all around Nina's abdomen, first high, then low, over to the right, then to the left, pressing harder, then pressing lighter. With every few seconds he seemed to be moving the device more quickly, searching more frantically. I lowered my head again and began to feel faint. *This is definitely not right,* I thought. *This does not feel right. Something is wrong. Something is wrong with the baby.*

"What's taking so long?" Nina said, with clear exasperation in her voice. "It never took Dr. Bowers this long."

I saw in Nina's face a look of intense fear. I could see that her lower lip was quivering, and that her breathing had become loud and fast. I could hear her heavy breaths from my chair in the corner.

I was feeling dizzy and somewhat distant. I almost felt detached from the scene, as though I was not really in the room with them. My head was light, my hands were wet with perspiration, and my stomach was tight as a drum. Everything now seemed to be happening in slow motion.

After what seemed like hours, but was probably only about another two minutes, Dr. Lloyd suddenly turned away from Nina and put his Doppler down on the counter.

"Well," he said in a subdued voice, looking down at the floor, "I can't find a heartbeat."

I heard his words, but they seemed like the script from some paranoid nightmare of mine. It didn't seem to me as though Dr. Lloyd had really spoken those words. I looked at him, and his tanned complexion seemed ashen as he wrote something in Nina's chart. I stood up and walked over to Nina, having to concentrate as I walked so I wouldn't stumble. She was lying down on the table, her stomach still covered with the KY Jelly. She was crying softly, with a distant, glazed look in her moist eyes. Her hands were at her sides. I reached down and grabbed her right hand and squeezed it. It was wet and clammy. Our eyes locked, and we shared a look of uncomprehending pain and terror, like animals caught in a trap. My eyes welled with tears.

I stood there for a moment and turned my head, staring blankly at Nina's stomach, as though I would be able to see something unusual or different from the way she had looked a moment before. Her stomach appeared exactly the same. I turned back to Nina and pressed her right hand with both of my hands. She inhaled sharply and closed her eyes tightly. Dr. Lloyd opened the door to the exam room and said something to Arlene, and then he turned around to us and said, "I want to take you next door to Dr. Thompson's office. He has an ultrasound machine there, and we can take a look."

I helped Nina up. On our way out we passed Arlene and Christine, who averted their eyes. We stepped out in the cavernous hallway, Nina slowly shuffling her feet as I held my arm around her, and then, into Dr. Thompson's office. The nameplate on the door said "Thompson Thompson, M.D." *How weird,* I thought, *his first and last name are identical.* I felt as though I was in the midst of a confusing nightmare.

Dr. Thompson met Dr. Lloyd, Nina, and me at the door and quickly walked us through his empty office to his ultrasound machine. Thompson was an older man, tall, thin, and bald, with a brusque manner.

"Lie down please," he curtly said to Nina. I helped her onto the table as Dr. Lloyd stood silently by. Nina was still quietly moaning and weeping as Dr. Thompson recoated her stomach with KY Jelly. I stood there feeling lightheaded and anxious, as I stared intently at the blank monitor on the ultrasound machine, hoping desperately that Dr. Lloyd had made a mistake.

As soon as Dr. Thompson placed the rounded wand on Nina's stomach, an image flashed on the ultrasound machine screen, but it looked just like static on a television to me. As Thompson adjusted a few knobs and moved the ultrasound device around a bit more, I could see the gentle profile of BJ's head. My eyes instantly moved to his chest, looking for the pulses of his heart, but all I could see was more static. We all stood there in tense silence for a few seconds. Then, without saying anything, Dr. Thompson slowly took a pen out of his pocket and pointed to the center of the screen.

"There," he said, expressionless. "There's the heart. It's not beating."

Nina closed her eyes and yelped sharply, as though she'd been stabbed by a knife. I stepped forward and stared at the screen, and I could just barely see a motionless, fuzzy oval shape.

"Are you sure?" I asked.

"I'm sorry," Dr. Thompson answered, his voice trailing away as he stepped back from the screen.

"Well, what can we do, what can we do?" I said, my eyes darting around the room. I expected them to begin massaging Nina's stomach to try to regain a heartbeat, or to call an ambulance, or to start rushing around the office preparing emergency shots. I was seized with a profound, indescribable sense of frustration and urgency.

"Let's do something now, can't we do something right now?" I shouted in a frenzied tone, turning around in a circle. Dr. Lloyd was standing next to me, motionless, as he stared at the ultrasound screen. Nina was softly weeping, her eyes closed. Her right hand rested limply atop her stomach. There was nothing we could do. BJ's heart had stopped beating.

Dr. Thompson walked out of the room, and Dr. Lloyd wiped the KY Jelly off of Nina's stomach. I helped Nina up. Her body was shaking slightly, and she had an absent look in her eyes. Her face was pale and her skin clammy. The three of us silently walked back to Dr. Lloyd's office. Nina continued her quiet cries. When we arrived in his office, he slumped behind his desk, and Nina and I sat in two large black leather chairs that were in front of it.

I began to feel angry. I had been in a kind of shock ever since Dr. Lloyd first had trouble finding the heartbeat. But now, as we sat in his office, I began to realize what had happened. Our baby had died.

I swore loudly. Already I was angry at God.

Nina had slumped down into her chair. She continued to cry, but she said nothing.

"I can't believe this is happening," I muttered over and over as I looked out Dr. Lloyd's window. He stared down at his desk.

After about five minutes, I sat up in my chair and said emphatically to Dr. Lloyd, "What on earth happened?"

"I don't know," he said simply, shaking his head. "Obviously something went very wrong."

"I can't believe this is happening, " I started repeating all over again. Nina had her hands in her lap. She was still shaking, head bowed, crying.

"What I'm most concerned about right now is you," Dr. Lloyd said, looking at Nina. "I want to make sure you have this baby as easily as possible. Just a minute please."

Dr. Lloyd called the hospital and swiveled around in his chair so his side was facing us. He began speaking quietly to someone. I scooted my chair over to Nina and kissed her forehead, then her cheek. She tasted salty from her tears. She turned and looked at me with an expression of heartbreak, ultimate heartbreak, in her eyes. There was a puzzled look on her face, but she couldn't say anything. She was still crying, and by now her face and eyes were red and puffy. Her body continued trembling.

I placed my right hand on her stomach, as I had been doing for nine months, and I kissed her cheek. I felt as though I wanted to pull BJ out of there and rescue him. But already a sense of finality had settled upon us.

What a horrible ending to our hopes and plans, I thought. *What a horrible ending for BJ.*

Dr. Lloyd was finishing up his conversation on the phone, and I thought about what I would say to him. I looked over at Nina. She looked markedly worse than she had just seconds before.

Dr. Lloyd hung up the phone and said calmly, "Well, that was the hospital. They're all set up for this, so it's basically up to you what you want to do."

"What do you mean? What are we supposed to do?" I said, bewildered.

"Well, I can induce Nina, or you can just wait a bit, or, if you insist, we could go ahead and do a cesarean on her."

"Listen." I leaned forward and addressed Dr. Lloyd with a firmness and intensity that surprised me. "We're thinking about the future. We need to do whatever it takes to maximize our chances of having a healthy baby in the future. We should deliver this baby in the way that is least damaging to Nina."

To this day I don't know where that remark came from. I was, like Nina, utterly stunned by the events of the previous few minutes. I had not thought about having children beyond BJ; indeed, BJ was all Nina or I had been thinking about. But I knew Nina and I wanted very much to have a family.

"I agree," Dr. Lloyd said. "I would be reluctant to do a C-section on her, and—"

"But we want to have this baby as soon as we can," I said, interrupting him. The thought of carrying BJ when we knew he wasn't alive was just too painful.

"I understand," he said. "Why don't you come back tomorrow morning, about 11:00 a.m. I'll check Nina, and then you can head over to the hospital about 1:00 in the afternoon. We'll begin induction of labor sometime that afternoon. How's that?"

"Fine," I said in a quick, barely audible voice, turning to look at Nina.

We sat there in silence for a moment, then Dr. Lloyd looked at both of us and said, "I'm sorry about this. Any number of things could have caused it; we'll do what we can to find out what it was. But, you know, this is a death in the family. You'll have to have some kind of memorial service or funeral. Do you have a priest or a minister or a rabbi?"

I paused for a moment. The word *funeral* rang in my head.

"Well, we're Christians, and we've got a pastor, but, I don't know, I don't know what we're going to do." My voice trailed away, as disbelief gripped me.

The thought of a funeral was so bizarre to me, so perverse. All we had done was go to the doctor's office for a checkup. There had been no explosion, no gunfire, no bleeding, no terrible disease, no car accident, no massive blow to the stomach. And yet, we were going to leave that office faced with the shattering reality of stillbirth and a funeral.

I glanced over at Nina, and she was looking still worse than before. She had pulled her feet up under her on the chair and was curled up into a ball, like a fetus. Her face had become very pale, and her cries had changed into what sounded like the whimpering of a seriously injured animal. *We've got to get out of here,* I thought.

"We'll think about that later," I told Dr. Lloyd, and then I got up and walked over to Nina.

Her body had grown rigid, and the tremors had become stronger. Dr. Lloyd got up and opened the door for us, and we slowly teetered out of his office and over to the front door. As we passed by the front desk, Christine was sitting there with her head down, resting it on her folded arms, as though she were hiding. Arlene stood behind her, off to one side, dabbing tears from her eyes. I had my arm around Nina as I opened the front door and looked out down the long stretch of foreboding hallway. As the door automatically closed behind us, its steely sound echoing down the corridor like the slamming of a prison door, Nina let out a groan.

"Ooohh," she said as though she had just been slugged in the stomach. I took a couple steps down the hallway toward the elevator, Nina's body leaning up against mine. She was barely able to walk. I had both arms around her as she leaned into me, and we slowly moved down the hall. With each step her crying became more intense. The dam had started to break. We were alone in the elevator on the ride down, and as we exited the building into the searingly hot southern California sun, Nina clutched her womb and began to wail.

"OH, MY GOD! WHAT HAPPENED? WHAT HAP-PENED? NO! NO!"

At once I wanted to join her in her screams, but I also wanted to get her home as soon as I could. A few people passed us in the parking lot with puzzled looks of horror on their faces. As we reached our Honda Civic, I opened the front passenger door and gently helped Nina into the seat. As her body dropped into the seat, she rolled over onto the driver's side, as though she had been shot. It was about 5:15 p.m., and I knew traffic would be heavy. I thought there was a good chance I would get into a traffic accident on the way home.

Looking back on that afternoon, I know without a doubt that I should not have been driving. I do not know why Dr. Lloyd let us out of his office that day; he clearly should not have. He should have called Nina's parents, who lived nearby, to come and pick us up.

But, like us, he didn't know what to do with this situation. He was a young doctor, probably about thirty-one years old, just getting started in his practice. He had never seen anything like this before, and he had no special training on how to deal with patients who come to the office and discover their full-term baby has died.

As I started the car and pulled out of the parking lot, I leaned forward to concentrate on the road, like an old man driving. Nina had sat up in her seat and was continuing to shriek at the top of her lungs.

"OH GOD, WHY? OH GOD, WHY?"

I reached over and put my arm around her back. She was rocking back and forth in her seat, her arms cradling her stomach, weeping with an intensity I had never seen in any human being before.

"I DON'T WANT TO HAVE THIS BABY! I DON'T WANT TO HAVE THIS BABY!" she yelled, violently shaking her head, gulping breaths between cries.

I didn't talk to her the whole way home as she continued screaming, saying those same things over and over. We were both deeply stunned. I reacted with silence, she with primal shrieks. I realized that our time at the hospital the next day was going to be a truly awful experience. *Where is God?* I wondered, as I stared at the road before me.

CHAPTER 4

A Night of Agony

*B*y the time we made it home after about thirty minutes of driving, Nina's crying had dissipated into the quiet tears with which it had begun. We walked into the house absolutely exhausted. I wanted only to lie on the couch and bury my head in a pillow, and I wanted Nina to do the same thing. But as we both walked into the kitchen, I realized that we would be unable to do that.

Coming out from a corner of the window sill and moving across the wall into the pantry were a pair of thick dark lines. Ants. Our kitchen was literally crawling with ants. I opened up the pantry and was confronted with thousands of ants crawling all around sugar, cookies, cereal, syrup, everything. They had also made their way down onto the floor. They were scouring it for crumbs and had formed a dense, dark line over to the small trashcan in the corner, which they had also conquered. Our kitchen had been over-run with ants while we were at the doctor's office finding out the worst news of our lives. Nina and I both stood there for a few seconds, our mouths agape. I thought we were the victims of an Old Testament plague. The thought ran through my mind: *God hates us, God hates us, and he is going to destroy us.* My soul winced at that lie, but in my anger and vertigo I didn't even have the strength to mutter, "Father, forgive me."

Before I could say anything about the ants, Nina walked over to the cabinet below the sink and began pulling out cleansers and rags. There was also a pair of yellow plastic gloves in there which I had insisted she wear every time she cleaned, so no chemicals or residues would seep into her bloodstream and hurt the baby. She reached for the yellow gloves out of habit, held them for a moment, then tossed them back into the cabinet.

She began furiously cleaning, spraying the ant lines with cleanser, and wiping them up with rags, sponges, and paper towels.

"Please call my parents and tell them what happened," she said to me through her sniffling.

I paused for a moment, wondering what I would say to them, and what I would ask them to do, but then I just punched their number in, figuring it didn't really matter how I told them.

Nina's father picked up the phone. A retired electrical engineer, he had never once shown any emotion. In fact, I found him to be a profoundly unemotional man.

"Joe, this is Brad," I said in a normal voice.

"Yeh, Brad."

"Listen, I, uh, I've got some bad news."

"Bad news?" he said, a little surprised.

"Qué?" I heard Nina's mother urgently ask in the background.

"Look, we couldn't find the baby's heartbeat at Nina's checkup today."

There was silence on the other end of the line.

"What happened, is Nina okay?" he asked, sounding confused.

"Well, she's here, but no, she's not okay," I said, my voice quivering.

"We're coming right over," he said firmly, and then, as he was hanging up the phone, I heard Nina's mother loudly ask, *"Qué pasó?"*

As I hung up the phone I looked at Nina, and she was sitting in the middle of the kitchen floor, surrounded by hundreds of little dead ants. I walked over to her and picked her up and hugged her. She cried nearly inaudibly as I hugged her. We stood there for a few minutes, still in shock from the news we had received nearly two hours ago.

"Go lie down, honey," I said.

She didn't say anything, and I led her over to the couch.

"Please call Susan," she said firmly.

"What for?" I said. Susan was the other teacher in her kindergarten class. They were partners teaching two classes in the same classroom, and Nina wanted me to tell her that she would not be in tomorrow or anytime soon.

Nina lay down on the couch and closed her eyes, and I went back over to the phone to call Susan. As I looked up the number, I realized I was going to have to call my parents. I didn't want to do that, but I knew the sooner I got it over with, the easier it would be.

I punched in Susan's number and told her directly as soon as she answered, "Susan, Nina wanted me to let you know that we went to her obstetrician today, but he could not find a heartbeat on the baby."

After a moment of awkward silence, Susan said flatly, "So, is that it?"

Taken aback by the sterility of her tone, I said just as flatly, "Yes, that's it," and hung up.

I was angry at Susan for her response, but as I later thought about that conversation, I understood that she simply did not know how to react. Who would? Unless someone has experienced a similar tragedy, or unless someone is uncommonly sensitive, they could not know how to react to such horrific news. Plus, my statement to Susan that the doctor "could not find a heartbeat on the baby" was somewhat ambiguous, especially to a woman who did not have children herself. Why had I not been more explicit? Because I simply could not bring myself to say directly, "Our baby is dead."

I then heard a knock on the door. I answered it as Nina stayed on the couch. It was her parents. Her father had a pained look on his face, and her mother, eyes red from crying, ran over to the couch and fell on top of Nina. They wept together, as her mother hugged her and said over and over, *"Oh, mi hijita! Oh, mi hijita!"*

"What happened, Brad?" her father said to me as I walked over to the phone again.

"I don't know," I said tiredly, shaking my head. "I have no idea."

I quickly punched my parents' number in, very much wanting to get it over with.

"Hello," my mother answered the phone.

"Mom, it's Brad."

"Yes," she said, surprised to hear my voice.

"Listen, I have some very bad news for you," I said in a rushed voice.

"Oh, oh, what is it?"

I could hear the fear in her voice.

"We just got back from seeing Nina's doctor, and there was no heartbeat on the baby. The baby didn't have a heartbeat."

"Oh, God! Oh!" she screamed into the phone.

"What is it?" I heard my father yell in the background. My mom continued screaming. I heard some fumbling on the other end of the line, then my father picked up the phone. "What is it, Brad, what happened?" he asked.

"Dad, there was no heartbeat on the baby today. Something happened to the baby." My mother had put down the phone, but I could hear her anguished screams in the background.

"I'm sorry about that," my dad said softly after a moment of silence. "Do you know what happened?"

"No," I answered. "We have to go into the hospital tomorrow and have the baby."

"Well, we'll be up first thing in the morning."

I said that was fine, then hung up as quickly as I could.

I truly dreaded having to see them after this, because I knew the pain and sorrow in their eyes would only intensify my pain. There would be, I felt, particularly on my father's part, an unstated and distant belief that somehow, this had been my fault. I had failed to manage the situation carefully enough. I had been careless. That was of course not the case. I knew that, and really, so did he. But his constant adjurations throughout the pregnancy to "take care of Nina" echoed in my mind, accusing me. The pregnancy of their first grandchild, my big chance to shine before my parents, had ended in disaster, and an inexplicable one at that. Knowing how my father's mind worked—he, like Nina's father, had been an electrical engineer—it would be important that there be an explanation for what had happened. I hoped Dr. Lloyd found some clear cause, or, I felt in some strange way, I would be guilty by default.

As that night wore on Nina and I were both restless. Her two sisters came over and tried to help her, but there was nothing to be done. They just sat around and cried. I wandered aimlessly around the house, and Nina lay on the couch. At about 8:00 p.m. her family left, and I helped Nina upstairs to bed. I was afraid she would not be able to sleep, but the trauma of the day had so drained her, she fell asleep with her clothes on. I went back downstairs and was alone for the first time that day. I headed to the refrigerator to find something to eat, only to be confronted by my prized eighteen-week ultrasound photo of BJ, which I had taped to the front of the refrigerator.

As I stood there staring at the picture, I muttered to myself, "I can't believe this has happened."

My eyes welled with tears as I realized, gazing at BJ's domed head and perfectly proportioned body, that he would not be born alive. He would not live. He would not live outside his mother, he would not be born into this world beyond the womb. All he would ever know was the dark, wet world of the womb. The life Nina and I had planned and imagined for him would not be. It would never be. Standing there, I felt as though I were beneath a dark, looming, malevolent cloud.

Now, the womb seemed to me a dangerous and threatening place. I felt like I should be doing something to rescue BJ, to make everything okay, and restore our world to what it was before we went to Dr. Lloyd's office earlier that day. But I knew I could not. So much had changed in the last six hours. Suddenly, a massive, utterly foreign shower of grief burst over me. I felt its chill, and my knees buckled as I moaned, "Ohhh!" and fell to the kitchen floor.

As I lay on the cold linoleum in a crumpled heap, I cried in a way I had never cried before. They were deep, body-convulsing cries that came in spurts, as though someone was intermittently kicking me in the stomach. I was trying not to make too much noise and wake up Nina, so I bunched my shirt up over my mouth, muffling my moans. Again, as I had felt in Dr. Lloyd's office during those hellish moments while he searched for BJ's heartbeat, it was as though I was not really there in the kitchen crying. My weeping sounded distant, as though it was coming from someone else. I imagined what I must look like lying there on the floor, utterly helpless and void of any hope.

After several minutes of tears, I felt Javert's coarse tongue lick my cheek. I rolled over onto my back as he continued lapping at my salty, tear-stained face. I sat up and rubbed his furry, fleshy throat, and looked into his soulful basset eyes. His naturally sad countenance now looked positively heartbroken, as though he shared my grief. I lay back down on the floor, which still smelled of the cleanser Nina had used to massacre the ants earlier that afternoon. I must have fallen asleep for a short while, because I was awakened by the ringing phone.

It was one of my brothers, Stan, who was five years older than I. He said he was sorry about what had happened and offered to come by and take Javert off my hands. Since I knew we would be gone for most of the next couple days, I welcomed the offer.

About a half hour later, Stan quietly knocked on the door. We didn't say much as he quickly led Javert out to his car. As he ducked into his car he turned to me and said, "I spoke to a friend of mine tonight who's a doctor, and she said what happened to the baby was probably a cord accident. She said that's what they call it, a cord accident."

I just nodded as though I knew what he was talking about.

Then he said, "Well, just try to put this behind you and get on with the rest of your life."

Swell, I thought. *What a great idea.* He meant well, but those words were completely meaningless to me at that time. And I sensed, however distantly, that ignoring BJ's life and death was not a path that would lead to any healing for Nina and me.

When I went back inside the message light was blinking on my answering machine. I pressed "play."

"Yes, Mr. Stetson," the pleasant female voice said with a thick English accent, "this is Jenny Howard at Travis Hospital. I'm the director of gynecologic nursing here. Dr. Lloyd called me today and told me of your tragic misfortune. I'm so sorry. Ring me when you get in, please, I have some important information for you about tomorrow."

I called her number and she instantly picked up.

"That was prompt, wasn't it," she said, sounding so proper.

"What will we do tomorrow?" I asked immediately, sounding every bit as helpless and hopeless as I felt. She gave me a detailed description about how to find the maternity ward, what to tell the nurses when I got there, and where in the hospital Nina would go after she had the baby.

Then she said, "Have you made funeral arrangements yet?"

My heart sunk.

"Uh, well, no, not really. I, uh . . ."

She jumped in, saying in a no-nonsense voice, "Well, you should start thinking about that, you know. Decisions will have to be made. By law you must provide some kind of burial plan. If you wish, the hospital will take custody of the remains, but you should think quite carefully about that."

I must not have sounded very alert, because her voice grew more intense.

"Brad, listen to me carefully. Listen. Tomorrow, when you and your wife go to the hospital and have your baby, it will be the hardest thing you have ever done. Do you understand that?"

I began softly crying. Her voice became tender.

"Dear, I just want you to prepare yourself. Try as best you can."

I choked out a weak "Thank you" and hung up the phone, only to lay back down on the chilly floor.

I snapped up nearly immediately though, when I heard Nina's strained voice calling me. I ran into the bedroom to find her sitting on the edge of her bed, with her arms around her stomach.

"I think I just had a contraction," she said with a worried and sickened look on her face.

"How do you feel?"

"Well, I don't know, I just feel all tight down there," she said, gesturing to her lower abdomen.

The teacher in the Lamaze class had told us to write down the times of each contraction once they started coming, so we would know how far apart they were. I didn't think there was much of a point in doing it now, but I went ahead anyway and picked up a pen and pad of paper. I lay next to Nina on the bed and wrote down the time of each contraction as Nina announced them. After a while, I had a long list: 9:30, 9:50, 10:12, 10:30, 11:00.

It was exceedingly painful for both of us to keep this list. With each entry, we felt again the stabbing pain of knowing our baby was not going to be born alive. A task that for most couples is an exciting one, a prelude to their trip to the hospital and the joyous birth of their treasured baby, was for us empty and tortuous. Each entry took us deeper into a pit of despair. I wanted to stop doing it, but I thought it might be important to be able to tell Dr. Lloyd or a nurse how far apart they were. So we drifted off to sleep, lying there in our clothes. With each contraction Nina mumbled, and I tiredly scribbled the time on the wrinkled paper.

We awakened the next morning at around 6:30, and as soon as I was conscious, Jenny Howard's words rang in my head: "When you and your wife go to the hospital and have your baby, it will be the hardest thing you have ever done." I lay there for a minute with my eyes wide open, staring at the ceiling, wondering if this was all a bad dream.

A heavy feeling of dread and nausea sat in my stomach. I didn't want to get out of bed, but as Nina started moving around, I knew we had to go through with it. We packed for the hospital, then went down and sat together on the couch, holding hands, trying to prepare ourselves for what lay ahead.

"How are you feeling, honey?" I asked.

"All right," Nina said. "Brad, why did this happen?"

"I have absolutely no idea. Obviously something went wrong."

"But we were so careful," Nina said, sounding exasperated. "We did everything right. I did everything I was supposed to do. I don't understand it."

"Nina," I said, trying to sound authoritative, "this didn't happen because you did something wrong, or because we were irresponsible or something. It just, it just, happened, you know. God has allowed this to happen to us." My voice trailed off at the end, my confusion cutting my explanation short.

After a while of silence I said to Nina, "When was the last time you felt BJ move?"

"Well," she said, pondering, "I was feeling him move all the time. I think the last time I actually remember him moving was on Monday night, when you came back from the walk with Javert and BJ gave that big kick when he heard your voice."

We looked at each other for a moment and then started crying profusely.

"He was saying good-bye to you, Brad!" Nina said, choking on her sobs.

We sat there and cried intensely together. On and on we went, for several minutes. Our joint sobs formed a tragic chorus, the inarticulate, tortured voice of our grief.

After catching our breath, we both leaned back into the cushions of the couch, already limp with fatigue, even though we had only been awake an hour or so. After several minutes we sat up, silently gathered our things, and left for Dr. Lloyd's office.

We weren't there for long. Christine was out somewhere, and Arlene led us straight back to an exam room when we got there. It was not the same room that had been our torture chamber the day before. The entire office now seemed like a sinister place to me. Nina and I both paced uncomfortably in the room. Dr. Lloyd walked in and asked us about the night before. I showed him the paper with the contraction times on it, but he ignored it. He then asked Nina to lie down, and he felt her stomach briefly.

"Well, the baby has dropped a little bit. Looks like you're ready. Why don't you try to get some lunch or something— eat light, though—and I'll call the hospital and tell them you'll be there around 1:00 p.m."

We wanted to get out of there quickly, so we were glad to be done in such short order. As we were leaving the office, Arlene was sitting behind the front desk. When we passed by her, she looked up at us and said, with teary eyes, "Good luck."

We both nodded at her and left the office, walking arm in arm down that cavernous, barren hall.

On the way to the hospital we stopped for lunch at a food court in a shopping mall. It was about 11:30 a.m. on August 14. Nina went to a table and sat down, looking forlorn. I brought over some soup and sandwiches, and we both sat there for a minute, looking at the people around us. Although we were in a loud and crowded mall, I felt completely alone. I felt almost alien, as though I were experiencing something no other person on earth had experienced.

And yet, surely many of these people had most likely suffered similar tragedies: infertility, miscarriages, the death of a child at birth, shortly after birth, or later in life. No doubt they had all suffered losses of some kind, because losing loved ones—and the intense, prolonged emotional pain and life-changes it brings—is an inevitable part of living and loving and being human. As the great Russian novelist Dostoyevsky wrote, "To live is to suffer." Thus the fact that we had experienced a deeply personal and tragic loss did not mean God did not love us, was not watching over us, or did not have important purposes for this particular experience; it only meant we were alive and engaged with this world, human beings encountering the inevitable tragedy of life. Our experience, though breathtakingly difficult, was one of the challenges God, in his wisdom and omniscient sovereignty, had allowed to come to us. As I scanned the crowd, I understood that each of these people knew, in their own way, the sting of death. I knew Nina and I were not the only people to suffer as we were.

But still, I felt separated from humanity and a common course of life. It was as though the unexpected death of BJ on the brink of his birth had diminished me irrevocably. The gruesome freshness of this loss had me in its disorienting thrall. I suddenly feared that I would not ever recover from this loss, that I would never live sanely or normally again.

Nina and I sat closely next to each other—like two lost campers shivering together in the wilderness on a freezing night—and ate in silence. Occasionally someone, usually an older woman, would walk by our table, notice Nina's large paunch, and give us a warm glance. This happened often when Nina was out in public, because she looked so cute being obviously pregnant. That happened two or three times that morning, but it was so painful we both instantly turned away from those congratulatory expressions.

Just as we were finishing and getting ready to leave, a young woman and a somewhat older woman—who, I assume, was her mother—walked past us. The younger woman was carrying a baby holder, and an infant who looked to be about one month old was asleep inside. As if directed to do so, they paused briefly in front of us, then walked on.

While they were stopped in front of us, reflexively, Nina and I leaned over to look at the baby. He was a beautiful boy wearing a little baseball suit. I turned to look at Nina, and she placed her head on my shoulder and began weeping very quietly. I put my head next to hers, and tears rolled down my face. We sat like that for about ten minutes, a sense of abject loss filling us.

We then rose from the table and walked out to the car with our heads down. I was consciously trying not to notice anyone around us, because I was afraid if I saw another baby I'd start crying, and that would make Nina cry, and our trip to the hospital would only be that much more painful. I felt the urge to pray, but in my exhaustion and depression, I could only think to myself, *Lord, help. Lord, help.*

CHAPTER 5

The Arrival of Grief

*A*s we headed into the hospital from the parking lot, we passed a minivan pulled up at the front door. A hospital attendant and a husband were helping a new mom into the van, with their most precious cargo already fastened into a car seat. Again I felt a sharp, piercing pain at the sight.

Better get used to it, I thought, *because we're going to see a lot of that around here.* How perverse and ironic that a scene of such beauty and sweetness would be so hurtful and difficult to behold.

We had to walk quite a ways to the maternity ward elevators. Jenny Howard had told me that the nurses' desk of the maternity floor was immediately to the right of the elevators. Sure enough, after the short elevator ride, in which Nina and I stood hand in hand in tense anticipation, the doors slid open and we stepped out, squinting under the bright lights. I looked to the right and saw the nurses' station, a bustling scene, with women dressed in hospital greens walking every which way.

Nina and I paused just outside the elevator. Nobody noticed us as we stood there. I was holding a small overnight bag, and Nina held a large white pillow. It must have been a common scene for a maternity floor. My heart quickened with nervousness as I looked around. I felt bewildered, and, like Nina, I was extremely anxious and fearful. But I knew nothing would happen unless I moved, so I told Nina to wait there, and, after drawing a deep breath, I started toward the nurses' desk.

I rapidly walked over to the desk. The nurse sitting behind it was bent over, writing something.

"Hi, I need help," I said in a pained voice.

"What is it?" the nurse said calmly, looking up at me.

She was about forty-five years old or so, with short blonde hair and a tanned, wrinkled face. I looked at her for a moment, thinking she might know who I was.

"Uh, well, we have a problem," I said haltingly. But then, regaining my composure, I said to her directly, using the exact words Jenny Howard told me to, "We've had a fetal demise."

"I know that," the nurse instantly answered back.

She and I looked at each other for a moment.

"Where's your wife?" she asked.

I gestured at Nina. "Over there."

As I turned and looked at Nina, my heart absolutely broke. She looked to me as sweet and beautiful at that moment as I had ever seen her. She was standing right where I had left her, clutching the big white pillow to her chest. She was resting her chin on it, and her big brown eyes were glistening, her tears reflecting the bright hospital light. Her round stomach was sticking out, speaking of the hope she had been cherishing these last nine months, and, indeed, her whole life. Her dark hair was combed down over her forehead, and the expression on her face was of profound hurt and sorrow. She was, in that moment, at once a vision of every woman's greatest aspiration and worst fear. As I looked at her, every cell of my body was filled with pain, and I wanted nothing but to hold her, and hug her, and try to comfort her.

The nurse came around the desk and said briskly, "Let's go." I motioned to Nina, and we followed the nurse down the maternity hall.

As we passed rooms on both sides of us, we could hear people talking excitedly inside. Some rooms had grandparents or friends standing in the doorway, with smiles of joy on their faces. As we passed one room we clearly heard the small but vigorous cries of a new baby.

The nurse took us to the very last room on the left. We were right behind her—hand in hand—as she walked in, pushed a curtain to the side, and turned on the light. She pulled a box of tissues out of the nightstand drawer and placed them on top. As she did that, Nina and I collapsed together onto the bed.

Immediately we both began sobbing uncontrollably. We were now holding each other on the bed, utterly bawling. A wave of grief and tears had swamped us, and we were both powerless to resist it. These were involuntary cries from deep, deep within us. As Nina and I lay on the bed, in a convulsing, sobbing embrace, the nurse stepped up to the edge of the bed. She leaned in over Nina's shoulder, just a few inches away from my face, which was toward her. She held up a button attached to a long electrical cord, and, pointing to it, said in a loud voice so I could hear her, "Press this button to call your nurse, okay? Use this to call your nurse!"

I nodded that I understood and continued my loud, uncontrollable howls. The nurse turned and quickly left the room, shutting the door behind her. As she left, I saw her bring a hand up to one of her eyes and dab at it. Nina and I continued to hold each other and cry vigorously, for about another twenty minutes. It was exhausting.

I do not know exactly why the walk to the room and our arrival in it had been so gut-wrenching for us. Perhaps because it was at that moment, as we entered the room, that the reality of what had happened—and what was going to happen—became a bit clearer. We had made our long awaited and long anticipated trip to the hospital, but it was under the worst possible circumstances. Our arrival in the birthing room, an experience which should have been exhilarating and joyous, was for us dark and foreboding, and only a further manifestation of all we had lost. Our son's birth seemed so much closer now, and along with it the searing agony we would feel at seeing and holding his lifeless body.

Although I didn't realize it at the time, the tearful embrace Nina and I shared on the bed seems significant for another reason. It was really the first time since we found out we had lost BJ that Nina and I truly began to experience the loss together. It was our entry into that birthing room—the place where our precious son would be born—that brought us, as a couple, into a union of grief and sorrow. We had, up to then, mainly experienced this as individual people and individual parents, persons whose separate lives had been scrambled in an instant. But now, in a setting where a husband and wife often have their most intimate and important experience as a married couple, Nina and I fully joined in our common suffering and shared loss.

After our tears subsided, we both felt drained but, oddly, somewhat relieved. The dreaded arrival at the hospital was over. We were there and could try to settle our nerves. I unpacked our bag, and Nina changed into a hospital gown. The birthing room was more like a hotel room than a hospital room, with *faux* hardwood floors, two large fabric chairs, a table, a television, and a large bathroom. After a few minutes there was a knock at the door.

"Hi, can I come in? I'm Corrie Van Dyke, your nurse."

The lady who came in, dressed in hospital greens, was about our age, with blonde-brown hair and dark skin. She immediately asked Nina if she could get her anything, and, after bustling around the room, pulled up a chair next to the bed and put her feet up on the bedrail.

"I'm sorry about what happened," she said matter-of-factly. "How'd you find out?"

This wasn't really a discussion we wanted to have, but she was so friendly and sincere, it was easy to talk to her. We told her we found out at our doctor's office. She said that just about two months earlier she had a miscarriage and didn't know about it until she went to her doctor's office when—she thought—she was eight weeks pregnant. She said she understood something of how we felt and ached for us. She spoke of two other women she had met in the hospital who had also had stillbirths. The stories she told were horribly sad, but, in a strange way, helpful to us. We learned other people had suffered as we had, but then had gone on to have normal lives—and healthy babies.

At one point Corrie asked Nina how she was feeling.

"Okay," Nina said, guardedly.

"No," replied Corrie quickly. "I mean, what are you really feeling like?"

"Well," Nina started slowly, "I feel like I've been run over, like I've just been flattened by a train, or something. I mean, I'm numb, in shock, everything has been happening so fast, it's like, an unbelievable nightmare. I can't believe I'm here, now, under these circumstances. I want to hold BJ, but I don't want to go through with the birth, you know, with all the pain and struggle, and then . . ." Nina's voice fell away as tears filled her eyes.

"I know it's going to be tough," Corrie replied casually. "You'll be pretty drugged up though; you shouldn't feel much physical pain at all." She sat there and talked with us a while longer, mostly about how her labors had gone with the two children she had.

Corrie was a big help to us. Although she didn't do much by way of physical or medical aid, the casual yet sensitive way she spoke to us for an entire afternoon put us at ease and calmed us.

Around 4:00 p.m. Dr. Lloyd came in looking dapper as always, even in his hospital greens. I had seen him walking around the maternity floor earlier that afternoon.

"I had some other work to do out here earlier today," he said, being careful not to mention that he had been delivering babies.

He felt Nina's stomach, then said he was going to break her water and begin induction of labor. He told Nina he thought it would be a good idea if she had an epidural to ease her labor pain and said the anesthesiologist would be by later in the evening to do that. After he broke her water and Nina was hooked up to various whirring and clicking monitors, we both tried to relax.

While Nina couldn't eat anything, I could, and was ready to get out of the room for a while. Corrie had given me a slip of paper with our room number on it and some other numbers and phrases, one of which was "fetal demise." She told me to take it to the hospital cafeteria for a meal.

I went down there around 6:00 p.m., and it was busy with the dinner crowd, a cross section of hospital humanity: excited kids, tired nurses, busy-looking doctors with beepers, administrators in suits, and the occasional forlorn-looking man or woman alone at a table, hunched over their food. As I got a sandwich and soda, I stood in line, waiting for the harried cashier to glance at my food. As I reached her, she leaned over to take a careful look at the slip of paper on my tray. She read it, looked up at me with a curious but sympathetic glance, and said, "Okay, go ahead," without asking me for any money. It was the first of many times in the hospital when people silently expressed condolences. It was an unspoken reminder to me of the gravity of the loss we had suffered, a gravity I did not yet fully comprehend.

When I arrived back in the room, Nina was asleep. I walked in quietly but tripped over an electrical cord, making a loud noise as my foot kicked her bed. She woke up and looked at me with a hollow gaze.

"What did you get?"

"A sandwich. Are you feeling anything?"

"Just some small contractions, nothing much."

I looked at her stomach to see if it seemed any different, but it was unchanged. Just then, there was a knock at the door.

"Hello, Nina?"

It was Nina's close friend Peggy. As soon as Peggy pulled the curtain back and saw Nina, she started crying. She walked over to Nina and kissed her on the cheek.

"It's okay, it's okay, Peggy," Nina said through tears, as the two longtime girlfriends hugged. Peggy was silent. She then sat down in a chair next to the head of the bed. As she started to cry again, she whispered, "I'm so-o-o sorry."

Peggy sat with us for about fifteen minutes, making small talk mostly. Clearly she was uncomfortable and didn't know what to say. There was not much to be said.

When Peggy left, we saw Tedi, our Lamaze teacher, leading a tour of expectant mothers and fathers around the maternity floor. We had grown attached to Tedi during our Lamaze classes and wanted to see her and tell her what had happened.

As Corrie led her into our room, I stood up and blurted, "Tedi, we found out yesterday our baby didn't have a heartbeat. Something went wrong."

She had not known us personally. We were just one couple among several in her Lamaze class, but she stood there stunned as I spoke, looking at Nina and me. Her gently wrinkled, grandmotherly face contorted into a sad frown, and she walked over to Nina and bent down and hugged her strongly, saying over and over, "You're in my heart, you're in my heart, you're right here in my heart!"

The three of us stood there for a moment with tears in our eyes, then Tedi quickly left, saying, "I've got to go; I'll be thinking of you dears."

The parade of people kept coming. Corrie came in with another nurse and said, "I'm off now. Nina, this is MaryAnn. She's going to be your nurse for the night."

Nina and I were both a little surprised. For some reason we had thought Corrie would be our nurse the whole time we were in the birthing room, but of course she had already been on for several hours before we got there that day, and now her shift was over. She hugged both Nina and me, and said, "Everything is going to go fine tonight, you'll see. You're going to be okay."

"Thanks so much, Corrie, we really appreciate your help," Nina said to her with obvious sincerity. "You were great."

MaryAnn walked over to the door with Corrie, and they whispered together for a moment, then MaryAnn came over and said to Nina, "Can I get you anything now?"

"No thanks, I'm fine."

MaryAnn put on a latex glove and said matter-of-factly, "Well, let me check your cervix just to see how dilated you are. We should start keeping an eye on that."

MaryAnn was a small, pale young woman with a sweet face and soft, Midwestern accent. She looked so small and frail herself, I wondered how she was able to do all the physical work of a labor and delivery nurse, but she seemed to know just what to do. She was obviously a person of unusual compassion and sensitivity. Everything about her spoke of kindness.

She pulled the sheet down below Nina's knees and quickly checked. "You're still only about one centimeter, you've got a ways to go yet." She covered her again with the sheet. "I'll let you get some rest now," she said as she left the room.

We had a few other visitors that night. My oldest brother Brian came by, along with his wife. They just stood around, mute with grief and inexperience with such catastrophes. Even our pastor, Ed, and his wife, Carla, who did have some familiarity with the tragedies which befall people, didn't know what to say when they visited us in the room that night. Nina and I were not the best of conversationalists at the time, either. It felt absurd to make small talk, yet Nina and I were so emotionally drained and numb, still shocked from the nightmare into which we'd been plunged, that neither one of us had the energy to think, let alone speak, coherently. But even so, it was comforting just to have their presence. The words people said were not really important, for their presence itself was a help to us.

Our last visitor that night was Jenny Howard, who came in around 9:00 p.m. As I had pictured her, she was a pleasant looking woman with brown hair, and even at the end of a long day, she had a perfectly pressed nursing uniform. She walked in briskly and said with her cultured English accent,

"Mr. and Mrs. Stetson, I'm Jenny Howard. I trust you are getting on okay?"

Nina, who was getting very tired and uncomfortable now, with her contractions becoming stronger and more frequent, grimaced a bit and replied, "We're okay, we just want to get on with this."

"I know, dear," Jenny said. "This is an extremely difficult time for you. Try to be brave. We'll do everything we can to help you. I want you to know that after the birth you'll come up to the fifth floor, the gynecologic patients' floor, and we'll keep you there at least a night just to make sure you're doing all right, okay love? Brad, will your and Nina's family be here tomorrow for the birth? Have you notified them all?"

"Well," I said, "Nina's parents live near by, so they'll be here, and my parents are coming up, but, uh, I'm not exactly sure when."

"Well," she said, sounding like an English school marm, "you really should call your parents and let them know Nina is going to have this child early tomorrow morning, so they can be here. You know, it will be important to them to be here. This is their grandchild. They'll be grieving, too."

At that moment I realized that our parents, families, and friends were in grief with us and would continue to grieve, as we surely would. Of course I should have known, but I was so consumed by what losing BJ meant to Nina and me, that I had not stopped to think about what it meant to my parents or anyone else.

Another woman came in and Jenny said, "Oh, Brad, I want to introduce you to Yvonne Salazar. She's a social worker here, and she'd like to talk with you."

"Hello, I am the bearer of juice!" the woman exclaimed, as she handed me a cup of cranberry juice. "I'm Yvonne. I'm a maternal social worker here, and I came by to chat."

She was short and chubby, with dark hair and a round face. She and I each pulled up chairs next to Nina.

"So," Yvonne began with purpose, "tell me about it."

Nina and I looked at each other. There was a moment of strained silence, broken when Yvonne urged, "Go ahead, tell me about it."

"Well," I began reluctantly, "there's not much to say. We, uh, just, are not doing too well right now. We . . ."

Nina could tell I really didn't feel like talking to this stranger, and apparently Nina didn't either, because she interrupted me and said shortly, "I'm sorry, but could we be alone? We don't really feel like talking now, you know. It's getting late and we have to rest. I know I sure do."

The social worker was taken aback and said in a slightly irritated tone, "Well, sure, if that's what you want. I'll just tell you what I tell everybody I work with: Trust yourself. You need to do that. Don't try to turn to some religious answer for this; don't think that God is going to get you through this. That's not realistic. Don't try to bypass yourselves. No, I want you to look to yourselves, just you two, and be real. You'll need to do that. Okay? You can call me anytime you need my help."

I nodded unenthusiastically, and Nina politely said, "Thank you for stopping by," and the secular social worker was gone.

"What was that for?" I said to Nina, after Yvonne was out of earshot.

Nina just rolled her eyes and turned over onto her side.

"Was that really her place to come in here and give us that little speech? Was that supposed to help us?" I said.

I was going to complain some more, but I noticed Nina was growing more and more uncomfortable. In fact, I was suddenly aware that Nina's face had grown pale and tight. She was grimacing in pain.

CHAPTER 6

He Is Perfect

I strode over to the call button and pressed it hard. Immediately a nurse said, "How can I help you?"

"We need to see our nurse," I said with a touch of urgency in my voice.

Within a minute MaryAnn came in, pushing aside the curtain that hung just inside the door.

"What is it, Nina?" MaryAnn said, looking concerned.

"I'm having a big contraction, it hurts pretty bad," Nina grunted, pronouncing the words in spurts.

"Let me check your cervix," MaryAnn said, as she put on a latex glove. "Mmm, you're about two now. That's good.

Let me get the anesthesiologist in here. You should have your epidural now, before you get any further along."

MaryAnn left the room, and I stood there holding Nina's hand. She still had a grimace on her face, and I could tell she was in considerable pain, even though, as was her habit, she tried to hide it from me, not wanting me to worry. I felt genuinely helpless standing there. She was lying right in front of me, experiencing considerable agony, and all I could do was stand there and look around the room.

"It's going to be all right, honey. MaryAnn went to get the anesthesiologist. He's going to be here soon," I said, trying to sound reassuring.

"Well, he better hurry up," Nina grunted. "I don't want to feel this anymore."

MaryAnn came back in the room. "All right, I've paged Dr. Brownson. He's on his way."

She started packing and unpacking drawers, placing towels on the bed, adjusting Nina's sheets, and generally being active. I paced around the room a bit and Nina writhed, rustling her sheets. After a couple more minutes Dr. Brownson walked in. He was a large, middle-aged, overweight man with tousled hair and a gruff manner. He sat by Nina's bedside and said brusquely, "Roll onto your side." As she did, he pulled up the back of her gown, exposing her back. I was looking over Dr. Brownson's shoulder.

As Nina lay there on the bed, exposed, I felt great sadness for her. She had the body of a woman nine months pregnant, but she would not enjoy the fruit of this pregnancy. She would not hold a live, kicking, cooing, wondrous baby. She would not enjoy the natural reward of all the physical pain and inconvenience she had endured, discomfort magnified for her because she had scoliosis—a crooked spine. This had made being pregnant and carrying extra weight even harder for her than it otherwise would have been. She had gained only about thirty pounds during this pregnancy, but since she started out at a petite ninety pounds, the difference was visible. As she lay there, I realized for the first time the extent to which being pregnant for nine months had changed her body. Hers was now a body ready to give birth—to nurse, to nurture, and to shelter a baby. Yet, she would do none of those things.

I watched as Dr. Brownson counted Nina's vertebrae, trying to find the proper spot to insert the needle for the epidural. It was a substantial needle; I was glad Nina couldn't see it.

"I see you've had some scoliosis," Dr. Brownson remarked casually. Then he said, a bit firmer, "You'll feel a stick here," and plunged the needle into Nina's back.

She twitched and moaned, then lay still.

Dr. Brownson leaned over Nina and—even though he had hardly talked to her at all while treating her—said tenderly, "It was nice meeting you."

Then, after a pause, he said, "I wish it were under better circumstances." He quickly walked out of the room.

After a few minutes Nina was feeling much better. It was now about 9:30 p.m., and things were quieting down in the hospital. There was less traffic in the hallway outside our door, and seeing Nina resting, I felt calm. MaryAnn came in and checked on Nina, felt her cervix, and turned the light down a bit, making the room darker, except for the glow of the television, which was on in the corner with the sound muted. Nina drifted off to sleep for a few minutes, as I just sat there wondering what was going to happen later in the night.

Nina woke up about thirty minutes later.

"How are you feeling?" I asked, placing my hand on her forehead.

"How long did I sleep?" Nina asked, looking alarmed.

"Just about a half hour; you're fine."

"I don't feel fine," she muttered. "Honey, why don't you just go home and get some sleep? There's nothing for you to do here."

"Nina," I said a little impatiently, "there's nothing for me to do at home either. I'll just stay here."

Nina continued to drift in and out of sleep, the anesthetic of the epidural making her feel drowsy. MaryAnn would come in and check on her periodically, and I just stood next to the bed, alternately glancing at the television and the other furnishings of the room.

By midnight I was starting to feel wiped out. I fell asleep in the chair next to the bed. Nina woke up and caught me asleep, and she urged me to go home for a couple hours and get some sleep.

MaryAnn had come into the room to check on Nina, and she said, "Go ahead on home, Brad. I've got your number. I'll just call you when she starts to get closer."

The thought of getting some sleep was tempting. When the traffic was light, as it would be now, we lived only fifteen minutes away from the hospital.

"Are you sure you want me to, honey?" I asked Nina.

"Yeah, go ahead, I just want to try and sleep."

So I left. I later regretted leaving because I learned—as I had suspected at the time—that Nina was in much more pain than she communicated to me. But the truth was I was glad to be going home, both for the sleep but also for a chance to be alone and try to understand what was happening.

When I got home, about twenty minutes after leaving Nina's bedside, our house was dark and still. It was nearly 1:00 a.m. It felt weird not to have Javert greet me as I walked in or to see him curled up in a large brown ball on the sofa.

I walked into the kitchen and put my keys down on the counter, and reflexively turned around to open the refrigerator, only to see BJ's ultrasound picture hanging on the door. I stared at it for a moment, again feeling the stab of reality. Without thinking much about it, I quickly took the picture off the refrigerator door and put it in a drawer beneath the counter. I listened to the messages on our answering machine. They were from friends, their messages essentially the same, as though they'd been reading from a common script.

"I found out what happened. I'm really sorry. Please let me know if I can do anything for you. I'll be thinking of you. Take care."

I appreciated those messages; it helped to know that other people were touched by BJ's life and loss.

I went upstairs planning to collapse into bed, but I passed by the baby's room, which Nina had so carefully prepared for BJ's homecoming. I felt irresistibly drawn into the room, although I knew what was going to happen while I was in there. I walked in and slumped into a rocking chair Nina's friends had bought her as a baby shower present. I sat there and looked around the room at the little stuffed animals, the clouds painted on the walls, the smiling sun. *This is a great room,* I thought. *Any baby would love this room.* I wept as I thought of the meticulous care and devotion Nina had shown in preparing it. My eyes paused on the framed needlepoint letters *BJ* hanging on the wall. We were going to give that to BJ when he was older, as a simple symbol of our devotion to him. I leaned forward in the chair, placed my head in my hands, and cried intensely.

Between sobs I looked up and saw the plain brown teddy bear, sitting regally on the table in the corner. Where before his visage had seemed peaceful and serene, he now seemed empty and still, his black eyes unreadable and mysterious. I began crying even harder and slumped to the floor. I felt a powerful pang of hopelessness slash through me, and I had no strength or will to resist the darkness it brought. For perhaps the first time in my life, I experienced true, complete hopelessness.

Christian writer Madame Guyon describes this state. She wrote, "Hopelessness constricts and withers the heart, rendering it unable to sense God's blessings and grace. It also causes you to exaggerate the adversities of life and makes your burdens seem too heavy for you to bear. Yet God's plan for you, and His ways of bringing about His plans, are infinitely wise."

But I did not feel as though any divine plan were at work in my life. I felt the unnerving and disconcerting threat of chaos.

"Why, why, why did this happen, God? Why did this happen?" I said, gulping air. I finished sobbing, and for several minutes I lay there on the floor hunched over, hearing only the crickets outside the window, their monotonous song filling the dark night.

By now the shock of the day before had abated somewhat, and while still stunned to be in this nightmare, my overriding emotion was pain. Intense pain. *BJ will not live,* I thought, *and all that his life might have been will never be.* I felt an aching emptiness, enveloped by despair. I lay there on the bedroom floor another half hour or so, alternately weeping and asking God why this happened, praying that Nina and I would find out what had caused BJ's heart to stop.

As I got up to leave, I realized that this room itself was going to be a source of pain. What had been planned as a sanctuary for our baby was now going to be a sinister presence. We would have to pass that room every time we entered or exited our bedroom. Would it be a constant physical reminder of how much we had lost, the childhood that would never be? As I walked out of the room I started to shut the door, but then I opened it all the way and left it open.

I awoke about two hours later to the ringing phone. I fumbled for the receiver, then placed it to my mouth and mumbled, "Yes."

"Hi, Brad, this is MaryAnn at Travis Hospital. Nina's going to have the baby soon. You can come down now."

Within five minutes I was in my car enroute to the hospital. It was about 3:30 a.m., and I made the trip in less than fifteen minutes. The humming of my car engine beckoned me to sleep, but I did not feel drowsy. I was unusually alert, adrenaline surging through my whole body. In the back of my mind there still lived an excitement at the thought of seeing BJ. Yes, he would be dead, but he would nonetheless be my son, and I yearned for him. I yearned to hold him and offer him up to God, as I had always dreamed I would one day do as a way of dedicating him to the Lord.

I parked and walked up to the entrance. The sliding doors didn't open, and I saw, in stenciled letters on the door, "This entrance closed from midnight to 6:00 a.m."

MaryAnn had not told me that I would be unable to use these doors, which were the main entry to the hospital. After knocking and knocking to no response—nobody was in sight—I started to panic. *I'm going to miss BJ's birth,* I thought, *and Nina will have to go through it without me.*

I screamed, "Hello!" hoping someone would miraculously appear and let me in, but the whole section of the rather large hospital was utterly deserted. I knew the twenty-four hour emergency room was on the other side of the building, so I started running around the perimeter of the hospital.

Travis Hospital was a large, ten-story building, with several small single-story buildings adjoining it, so I had a ways to jog, probably about one-third of a mile. The cool night air, driven by a slight breeze, stung my face as I ran. I was clutching a pillow Nina had asked me to bring for her. As I approached the emergency room, I realized I was going to have to ask someone in there for directions to the maternity floor, since it was nowhere near the emergency room in this sprawling hospital.

I ran into the open doors of the emergency room without even slowing down, startling the few nurses and attendants who were just standing around the empty area. They all looked at me with surprise, as I said in an urgent and winded voice, "Where's the . . . where's the labor and delivery floor? I need to find labor and delivery."

A couple of the people started pointing in various directions and giving conflicting instructions.

I looked frustrated and snapped, "What?" Then a young male orderly came out from behind a counter and said, "I'll take you there, follow me," and we both jogged down a hall, away from the emergency room.

As I started leaving, I glanced at the other emergency room workers, who were laughing. I must have looked like quite a sight. The nervous and frazzled father-to-be, holding a big pillow, running around frantically looking for the maternity floor. Of course they didn't know my particular circumstances, but their laughter—which was no doubt meant in good humor—was painful to me, because it reminded me of what a joyful time this was supposed to be and what an awful thing had happened to us. I felt an urge to yell at them, "He's dead! He's going to be born dead!" But instead I kept silent and followed after the man escorting me.

"Okay, there, right up ahead, see?" the young man said, pointing to a bank of elevators about sixty feet away, down a hall. "They'll take you up to labor and delivery. Good luck, man," he said as he jogged passed me, on his way back to the emergency room.

"Thanks," I said quietly.

I exited the elevator and walked onto the maternity floor, which was nearly empty. I strode down the hall, again hearing the irritated cries of a newborn baby, and walked into Nina's room. MaryAnn was seated, writing something, and Nina was sitting up a little, wiping her eyes with a tissue. I could tell she had been crying.

"What is it, honey?" I said as I grabbed Nina's hand. She didn't say anything.

MaryAnn said, "I've called Dr. Lloyd. He'll be here shortly, and then pretty soon Nina can start pushing. She's about seven centimeters dilated now. I don't think she's too far away." Then she left the room.

I turned back to Nina. "What is it, honey? Tell me what's wrong."

"While you were gone," she started, but stopped, overwhelmed with tears. I sat next to her on the side of the bed, holding her hand. I bent down and kissed her cheek.

"While you were gone," she began again, still crying, "all I could hear, all I could hear were babies crying. I heard newborn babies crying!"

She was now sobbing heavily. I lay by her side and put my arms around her.

"I know, honey, I heard them too," I said through tears.

We both lay there crying together for several minutes. Then I said, "I know it hurts, honey. I know it hurts." I was groping for words, wishing I had something healing to say.

Nina wiped the tears from her now red nose and face, and said, "It more than hurts. I can't stand it. It hurts me too much to hear that. We've got to keep the door closed from now on."

I got up and closed the door. As I did so, it occurred to me that the pain of this loss was not going to be so easily avoided. There would be no door to close to keep the agony away, for the agony would be inside us, in the very center of our being. BJ was our son, and many months ago his life had been forever wedded to ours. I knew, however faintly, that Nina and I would have to accept this torment, and allow it into our souls, and not try to shut it out. We had been set on a course of existential change, for better or worse, and we could do nothing to stop that.

A few minutes later MaryAnn walked in with Dr. Lloyd right behind her.

"How are you guys?" Dr. Lloyd said as he put on a pair of latex gloves.

"Okay," I said. Nina didn't say anything.

"Did you just get here, Brad?" Dr. Lloyd glanced at my disheveled clothes and hair.

"Uh, yeah," I replied sheepishly. "I had to run around the perimeter of the hospital to get in, because the main doors were closed."

MaryAnn turned to Dr. Lloyd with a look of "Oops" on her face, and Dr. Lloyd scowled at her.

Then Dr. Lloyd walked over to Nina. "Okay, I want to see what your cervix is like."

He pulled her sheets down.

"Good," he said after a few seconds, "your cervix is soft, and you feel like you're about at eight centimeters. I'll be back in a few minutes, and then we'll start pushing. You're almost there, Nina, hang in there." Dr. Lloyd pulled off the gloves, tossed them into the trash can, and left.

I leaned down and kissed Nina as she started to cry. "It's okay, honey, it's gonna be okay. We're going to have BJ soon," I whispered.

"I'm sorry," Nina said through tears, "I'm sorry you won't have your boy, honey. I wish you were going to."

We hugged, kissed, and cried for another minute or so, then Nina said in a surprisingly firm voice, "Brad, call my parents and your parents, and tell them that we're going to have BJ soon. Your parents are going to have to leave their house soon to get here to see him, and I want my mom and dad to be here, so please call them."

I called Nina's parents first. Her dad's groggy voice answered. "Qué?"

"Joe," I said clearly, "Nina's going to have the baby soon. You can come down any time."

"How is she doing?" he asked.

"She's fine, I guess. She's going to start pushing now though, so you can come on down."

"Okay, we'll be there soon," he said.

Then I called my parents and had the same conversation with my dad. As I was talking with him I heard my mother urgently ask in the background, "What's going on?" My dad said to her, "Nina's starting to push," then he said to me, "Okay, we'll be up in about two hours or so."

Just then MaryAnn started moving a lot of equipment in the room, and I told my dad I had to go.

The room was being transformed before our eyes from an imitation hotel room to what looked like an operating theater. A light came down from the ceiling, part of Nina's bed folded under itself, and a long tray with various instruments on it was placed next to Nina's bed. MaryAnn was still busy populating this tray with unfamiliar looking tools, when Dr. Lloyd walked in wearing surgical greens.

"Okay, Nina," he said, leaning into her. "I'm going to ask you to start pushing now. We're going to have you push as hard as you can for ten seconds, then pause, then push again, okay? How much pain are you feeling right now?"

"None," Nina said, sounding drowsy, "my whole lower body is numb."

I stood next to Nina on her left side at the head of the bed, with Dr. Lloyd sitting in front of Nina and MaryAnn on the other side of her. I grabbed Nina's left hand and said to Dr. Lloyd, "What should I do?"

Dr. Lloyd was adjusting Nina's legs in the stirrups and didn't answer me at first. Then he looked up at me and said, "Why don't you do the counting."

Then he pulled his stool closer to Nina and said in a strong voice, "Okay, Nina, I want you to push as hard as you can. Go."

"Come on, Nina!" MaryAnn said firmly.

"One, two, three, four, five . . ." I counted, trying to stay in time with the second hand on my watch.

"Good," Dr. Lloyd said.

"Aahh!" Nina screamed loudly just before I reached the count of ten.

"Try not to scream or grunt too much, Nina, your push will be stronger if you don't," Dr. Lloyd said.

"Right, I'll do that," Nina answered sarcastically.

We paused for about thirty seconds and then started again.

"Push!" Dr. Lloyd commanded, and Nina's face turned red with strain. She was squeezing my hand hard with her left hand, and with her right hand she was squeezing one of MaryAnn's hands. Her knees were pulled up close to her chest.

"One, two, three, four, five, six . . ." I announced, with a strength that surprised me.

"Good, you're making progress," Dr. Lloyd encouraged, as he placed a hand lightly on top of Nina's stomach. I looked down at her stomach, and it seemed as though it had changed shape slightly. The baby was clearly down low in her uterus, and it seemed to me from where I was standing that her stomach was not symmetrical. One side of it looked higher than the other side.

"Aahh!" Nina exclaimed again, as we reached the count of ten.

"You're doing good, Nina, keep trying," MaryAnn said heartily.

After a few seconds Dr. Lloyd said, "Okay, this time, Nina, when you're pushing, I want you to breathe out really strong. Exhale as strongly as you can."

Remembering our Lamaze class, I reached into our overnight bag and pulled out our "focal point" for labor. It was supposed to help Nina concentrate. It was a small, soft, green and yellow car that made a honking noise when squeezed. It had a license plate sewn into it which read, "Baby One." We had planned on giving it to BJ. Before I put it in front of Nina, I hesitated, wondering if it would be painful for her to see it. But the Lamaze teacher said it was important we have a focal point, so I went ahead and put it on Nina's chest as I grabbed her hand, getting ready for her to resume pushing.

"Put that thing away," Nina said immediately.

It was too painful a reminder to her of BJ and all our plans. I turned around and buried the car in the overnight bag, regretting not having trusted my intuition.

"Push!" Dr. Lloyd exhorted, as I grabbed Nina's hand. Her face again contorted, and she made a loud "Shhh" sound as she exhaled hard. It looked as though every muscle in Nina's face and arms was tense as she ground her teeth and pushed.

"There you go, Nina," Dr. Lloyd urged, "push hard."

I began reciting, "One, two, three, four, five, six, seven," as MaryAnn squeezed Nina's other hand and wiped perspiration off her forehead.

"Okay, I can tell you're getting there, Nina. A few more good pushes and you should be there," Dr. Lloyd said, with a touch of excitement to his voice.

As Dr. Lloyd spoke those words, Nina and I looked at each other with an odd combination of excitement, fear, and sadness. A moment we had dreamt of was about to be upon us, and yet, we knew it would be unbearably painful. Dr. Lloyd turned and said something to MaryAnn who left the bedside momentarily and returned with what looked like a pair of scissors. Nina and I both glanced at it, wondering what it was for. Then Dr. Lloyd again leaned in toward Nina's midsection, and said slowly, "Nina, when I say, I want you to give me your strongest push yet." He paused, then looked up at her and said with raised eyebrows, "Okay, get ready, go!"

"One, two, three, four, five, six, seven, eight," I said loudly, counting slightly faster than before.

"Come on, Nina, you can do it!" MaryAnn cheered.

"Push strong!" Dr. Lloyd said sternly.

"There, all right, you're starting to get a little bit of the head. Nina, keep pushing." Dr. Lloyd picked up what looked like a suction cup.

He reached in toward Nina and appeared to attach the cup to something, but from where I was standing, I could not see what he was doing.

When Dr. Lloyd said he saw a bit of the head, my heart fluttered and my stomach sank. Nina squeezed my hand even tighter. Both of our hands were partially white from the pressure of our squeezing.

After a few seconds, MaryAnn said, "You're going to get him this time, Nina, I can feel it, you're going to do it now!"

I felt tears starting to well in my eyes, as I realized BJ was about to be born. The time had come. Nina slid down a bit in her bed, and tucked her chin into her chest, tightening her grip on my hand and MaryAnn's hand.

"When I say, you're going to give it your best push," Dr. Lloyd said to Nina, punctuating the end of his sentence by making a punching motion with his closed fist. "Ready, get set, do it!" Dr. Lloyd yelled.

"Go ahead, honey," I said through tears, my voice wavering, "push as hard as you can."

I was about to start counting again, when Dr. Lloyd said in drawn-out words, "There you go, that's right. Come here, Brad, look at this."

I stepped to the foot of the bed and leaned over, looking in over Dr. Lloyd's right shoulder. BJ's head was halfway emerged. It seemed somewhat gray and ashen in color, moist with fluid and blood. He was face down, the thin blonde hair on the back of his head matted with moisture. The four of us were silent as Dr. Lloyd gently grabbed the side of BJ's head and eased it the rest of the way out. When I could see his full head, I recognized the slope of his forehead from the ultrasound picture we had been viewing for months. As Dr. Lloyd wiggled the base of BJ's head a bit, to bring the shoulders through, the rest of him slid out, making a sort of slurping noise as the full body emerged. As I stood completely transfixed, I noticed the umbilical cord. It was wrapped tightly around BJ's neck several times, looking very much like a noose. I was struck by how thick and strong the umbilical cord appeared. It was muscular and sinewy, sort of a pale blue and off-white in color. It was clearly very long. Nina was trying to raise her head so she could see, but she was unable to catch a glimpse of BJ at first.

"Here he is, honey," I said through tears, moving toward the head of the bed. I leaned in to her. "Here's BJ!"

I placed my hand on her chest, clutching her hand in mine, as Nina craned her neck and said urgently, "Let me see, let me see him."

Dr. Lloyd held BJ up a little bit, holding him under the shoulders. Nina's mouth formed a half smile, then she closed her eyes and began weeping, her head falling back into her pillow. I bent down and kissed her.

"I love you, Nina," I whispered as I wiped perspiration off her forehead with my hand.

I then turned to look at BJ. Dr. Lloyd was holding him in his arms, wiping some blood off his face. I walked closer as Dr. Lloyd stood up. Cradling BJ with his left arm, he began, using his right hand, to slowly unwrap the umbilical cord from around BJ's neck. Dr. Lloyd had a truly mournful look on his face as he did this. His eyes welled with tears as he methodically moved his right arm around and around, unwrapping the cord about four revolutions.

"It's so thick and big," I said in amazement, as I stared at the cord. I was struck by how thick the cord was compared to BJ's neck. They were nearly equally thick, BJ's neck only slightly more so. The sight was a brutal one. The cord looked to me like a malevolent creature, a sort of giant snake. It seemed so coarse and rough, and it had easily throttled BJ. I felt great sorrow and helplessness viewing this scene, and was filled with an intense desire to rescue my son, but I could not do so. My heart was at my feet.

"Oh, BJ, oh, BJ," I said in a low, mournful, pained voice.

Nina was still crying, intermittently opening her eyes and craning her neck to see BJ.

"The cord choked him, didn't it, Dr. Lloyd," I said, with a tone of finality to my voice.

"Here, look at this," Dr. Lloyd said, holding up with his right hand a portion of the umbilical cord that was closer to the placenta, which was now dangling out of Nina. "Do you see this?" He held between his fingers a section of the umbilical cord that had formed a large, tight knot. "This is what did it."

"Is that normal?" I asked, knowing the answer.

He shook his head. The knot looked like a big ball of cord, about the size of a billiard ball, but it was only a single tie, as though the cord had formed a loop, and then one end of it—the end attached to BJ—went through the loop, forming a knot. I was particularly struck by how tight the knot was. It could not have been tighter had it been deliberately tied by a very strong man.

As I stared at the knot, I realized I was looking at the cause of my son's death. The knot had cut off his oxygen supply. Involuntarily, I began gushing tears.

"It was the cord, honey!" I said in a loud voice to Nina through my tears. "There was a knot in the cord; that's what did it!"

I bent over and kissed and hugged Nina as we both cried. After a few seconds I stepped back to where Dr. Lloyd was standing with BJ and said to him, "What could have caused a knot like that?"

Dr. Lloyd was still holding BJ and looking at the cord. He shook his head and sighed. "I don't know. The cord looks rather long to me. I'll be sending it to the lab, anyway, so we might find something out."

He then picked up the surgical scissors that had been on the tray. Holding BJ in his left arm, he offered the scissors to me. "Do you want to cut the cord?"

I was not expecting him to ask me that question. I had not even realized the umbilical would need to be cut. I hadn't thought that far ahead.

Without thinking, I said, "No."

Dr. Lloyd looked disappointed. He picked up the scissors and, squeezing them hard, cut through the thick, muscular cord with one clean stroke. The long cord dropped onto Nina's bed.

I instantly regretted not cutting the cord. Had I done so it may have been a rich symbol of the intimate union of Nina, BJ, and me, with me, his father, separating him from his mother and receiving him into our arms. I wish I knew why I declined to cut that cord. If I had thought about it ahead of time, perhaps I would have been alert enough to say yes to Dr. Lloyd's offer.

After Dr. Lloyd had cut the cord, he began to tie off the umbilical cord near BJ's belly. He turned around to MaryAnn, about to ask her to get him something, but she was now standing in the corner of the room, quietly weeping, her hands covering her face. Dr. Lloyd paused for a moment, looking at her, and then said sharply, "Nurse."

MaryAnn looked up and wiped her face with her hands. Nina said to Dr. Lloyd, "Hand him to me."

During the few minutes that had passed since the birth, Nina had been overwhelmed with grief and very much weakened by the anesthetic she'd been given, as well as by her labor—even though her actual pushing lasted only about twenty-five minutes.

Dr. Lloyd passed BJ off to MaryAnn, who was holding a blanket. She quickly wrapped him in the blanket, put a small light blue cap on his head, and handed him to Nina. Her tired and limp arms did not look like they could hold BJ, but Nina received him like an experienced mother, and drew him to her chest. Since his neck was limp, his head flopped over onto Nina as she pulled him closer to her. I stood next to Nina, my right hand behind her head, as she sat up in bed, cradling BJ in her arms. She was looking down at him with a look of absolute anguish on her face. The center of her nature as a woman was to nurture her child, and now, she held in her arms her baby whom she would not suckle, her son whom she would not raise, and her young man who would never be. As she gazed at him with a love and longing that cannot be put into words, the depth of grief that filled her eyes revealed a piercing awareness of her loss.

I moved my eyes from Nina and looked into BJ's eyes, which were half open. I saw that they were light hazel in color, like my father's.

"He looks like my dad, Nina," I said in amazement.

"He does, he looks a lot like him, especially around the jaw and mouth," Nina said slowly, gently rubbing her right hand down one side of BJ's face.

His skin was pale in color, with what looked like a lot of red blotches. His rib cage seemed a bit askew, as though it had been dislocated or something. There seemed to be a certain lopsidedness to his appearance. Blood had pooled in his extremities, so his fingers had a strange red tint at their tips. So did his eyelids.

"His hands are so big, Nina," I remarked, pulling a limp left arm out from the wrap.

"He has your hands, honey," Nina said, gently taking the hand into hers. She held the hand tenderly, carefully studying it. She brought BJ's hand up to her lips and softly kissed it. I leaned over and kissed the hand as well, as Nina continued to hold it.

"His hair is so light; why is his hair so blond?" Nina asked. Neither Nina nor I had light hair, yet BJ did.

"I had red hair as a baby, Nina, that must be it," I told her.

"Yeah, but this is blond. It's so cute."

"Pull his blanket back, honey, let's see his other arm," I said, feeling excited, as though we were unwrapping a long-anticipated, treasured Christmas gift. Nina pulled the arm out. Like the other, it was beautifully formed and utterly complete.

"He's perfect, honey," I said to Nina, tears coming back.

"He is perfect. He looks just like his daddy."

Nina then turned BJ around on her chest, so that he was now facing us. She was holding him up a little bit, so that it looked as though he was standing on her chest. The blanket was still covering his back and lower body. His full upper body was before us. It was thin and wiry, and it looked as though it had been through a lot. There seemed to be small spots of bruising or discoloration scattered across his chest and abdomen. We could clearly see his ribs, pressing up against his chest, on one side of his body. His vacant eyes were half open.

"Close his eyes, Brad," Nina pleaded.

I gently placed my index finger on top of each eyelid and pressed them closed. He looked peaceful in his mother's arms now. His mouth was slightly open, as though he was breathing through it.

"We love you, BJ." Nina started to cry gently.

"Let's see his legs," I said tearfully, as I pulled them out from the wrap. They were thin and pale but perfectly formed.

"Look how big these feet are, Nina," I remarked, as I picked up BJ's right foot. It was a perfect baby foot, surprisingly long. The tips of his toes were red with pooled blood. It did not look normal.

"Look at these precious little toes," Nina said through tears, as she put two of her fingers beneath them and rubbed BJ's little rounded, red-tinted toenails.

During this time Dr. Lloyd was still seated at the stool working, and MaryAnn was moving around the room. Her eyes red from crying, she said in a near whisper, "I'll measure him, take a few pictures for you, get footprints, hand-prints, and a lock of hair for you, whenever you want."

I nodded at MaryAnn, and she turned around. Then Nina lifted BJ up a bit and said, "Honey, hold him."

I reached down, and, holding him under the arms, pulled him close to me. I had literally never held a baby before. I hadn't even held friends' babies, because I was too worried I would drop them. I felt unsteady and awkward as I took hold of BJ.

"Hold him underneath, honey," Nina said, making a cradling gesture with her arm.

I placed my left arm underneath BJ's bottom and my right hand on the back of his still moist neck as I brought him to my chest. I closed my eyes and squeezed him slightly. His limp neck did not support his head, and the weight of it rested on my chest. I stood there with my eyes closed, concentrating on the feel of his head on my chest. It was a soft pressure, a subtle pressing, which could easily be missed. But it was a wonderful feeling to me. As I stood there for a moment, eyes closed, I let myself imagine that he was alive and sleeping in my arms. My eyes began brimming with tears again, as I lifted him up slightly, held him out from my chest, and looked at his face, which was hard to see because his head had slumped down. I held his chin up with my right hand and studied his face. I saw my father's face. BJ's face—its shape, jawline, complexion, and proportions—looked strikingly like my father's.

I was, at that moment, filled with a tremendous sense of pride. I was proud of BJ, proud he had been born, proud I had a son. It was a tremendously exhilarating feeling. I half felt like striding out into the hallway and going door to door, showing him off.

"He looks good, I think," I said aloud, still studying his features.

I turned to Nina to see her reaction, but her eyes were closed. "Honey," I said, but she didn't respond. The drugs and the stress of the ordeal had exhausted her, and she was soundly asleep. I rewrapped BJ in his blanket and sat in a chair next to the bed, feeling strangely relaxed and relieved.

After a few moments I looked around the room. Dr. Lloyd was still sitting at his stool in front of Nina, silently working, eyes downcast, and MaryAnn was standing at the back of the room, next to a warming table—a holder for newborns. I walked over to her and asked, "Can you take some pictures, MaryAnn?"

"Sure, let me get the camera," she said as she turned around. I don't know why I hadn't brought my own camera. I later very much wished I had, as those few pictures of BJ MaryAnn took are priceless to us.

She snapped a few pictures of me holding the baby and a few of him lying in the warming table. Then she weighed and measured him. He was only four pounds fourteen ounces and about seventeen inches long, but Dr. Lloyd told us he would have been about an average-sized full-term newborn, without the cord knot. It was now nearly an hour since BJ had been born, and Dr. Lloyd was getting ready to leave.

"Brad, I'll be back early this afternoon to check on Nina. She'll be on the fifth floor then." He patted me on the shoulder and left the room, his surgical greens stained with blood.

MaryAnn handed BJ back to me. "I'll leave you and Nina alone now, okay? You can have some time alone with the baby."

She left, pulling the curtain and door closed behind her. I walked back over to Nina. She was still sleeping. As I walked around the room holding BJ, I felt unexpectedly relaxed and unburdened. I carefully studied his face, his thin, curly blond hair, the splotchy marks on his body, his little button nose, his arms and legs, and his crooked chest. I kissed his forehead and rubbed his cheeks and the top of his head. *What an amazing thing he is,* I thought. I knew he was the product of sexual intercourse between my wife and me, but I found that hard to believe as I beheld him. He seemed far too complex and intricate to have been naturally assembled inside of Nina's body. *What a miracle he is,* I mused.

"Oh, BJ," I cooed at him, "Mommy and Daddy love you soooo much. We love you very much."

I started to cry involuntarily again, but it was a dry cry; I had no tears left to shed. I slumped down in the chair, put BJ on top of my chest and stomach, and closed my eyes. I again concentrated on how he felt lying on top of me. *I never want to forget this feeling,* I thought. I sat there in silence as Nina slept.

After a few minutes MaryAnn came in quietly. She approached me and said softly, "Brad, have you thought about baptism? The chaplain is waiting down at the nurses' station if you want him to come in and baptize the baby."

As with so many other things, baptism had not crossed my mind. "Well, sure," I said, "Let me wake up Nina for this."

I walked over to her and shook her gently, "Honey, wake up, the chaplain is here, he's going to baptize BJ for us."

"Huh?" Nina said drowsily, waking up.

"Sit up, Nina," I said, as the chaplain walked in the room.

He was an elderly man, probably in his early seventies, with a hunched back and slow, shuffling walk. He had a full head of hair, which was white, and even more disheveled than mine. He also had on a clerical collar and wore a large wooden cross around his neck.

"I'm Chaplain Mathis," he said, as he looked at Nina but stuck his hand out in my direction.

I shook his hand and said, "Thanks for coming," but before I had blurted out those few words, he had already brushed by me and was standing at the head of the bed next to Nina. I had given BJ back to her when she woke up, and she now held him in her arms.

"Is this the little critter?" the chaplain said, leaning in for a better look. "He looks like dad," he remarked casually. Nina and I exchanged smiles. "I'm sure you'd like to be alone, so let me get on with it," the chaplain said, as he pulled out of his shirt pocket a small glass container of water.

"Yes, Almighty God, I baptize this child in your presence and ask your blessing on him," the chaplain said, as he wet his fingers and momentarily pressed them to BJ's forehead. He continued in a voice so casual, I nearly thought he was talking to me.

"You know, Lord, what it is to lose a son, to suffer loss. You know the darkness and despair we face. May your hand guide this family, may your grace rest upon them, and may their future be blessed by the fulfillment of your purposes and by your merciful love."

He paused for a moment with his eyes closed, and then opened them. He looked at me and said, squinting, "What is the child's name?"

"Uh, it's BJ," I said leaning toward him, as though he were hard of hearing.

"Almighty God, may BJ be with you forever and ever, and may the seed of his young life cut short yield in the fullness of time a maturity and peace in the lives of his parents that is pleasing to you, and that allows them to be a comfort to others who have suffered as they have. In your Son's precious name, amen."

And then, as suddenly as he had come, he turned to leave. As he was shuffling out of the room, he turned around and said to Nina and me, with a raised and slightly shaking right hand, his index finger pointing upward, "I know you folks can't imagine this now, but you'll get through this, you'll see. In time, you'll see what I mean; just persevere. God never gives you a mountain to climb without also giving you a good pair of boots to do it with." After turning around to leave, he said, waving his finger back at us, "Things will work out someday, you'll see. They always do."

Then, as if it was some slapstick routine, the old chaplain inadvertently opened the door to the bathroom. "Ahh!" he said, startled, as he closed the bathroom door and walked around the curtain to the correct door, leaving the room.

I stared at the door after he left, struck by the beauty of his words, but too dazed to really appreciate them. "What a character," I said to Nina.

"I liked him." Nina smiled, kissing BJ's forehead.

MaryAnn then pushed the door open a little bit, stuck her head inside, and said, "Nina, your family is here, down at the nurses' station. Shall I send them in now?"

Nina turned and looked at me with a look of sad apprehension on her face, then she said to MaryAnn, "Go ahead and send them on in."

Nina's mother walked in first, followed by her father, two sisters, and brother. The whole family had come. Nina sat up in the bed, holding BJ, as her mother walked over to her, weeping.

"Oh, *mi hijita*," she said, kissing Nina on the forehead.

Nina pulled the sheet away from BJ's head so her mother could see him. Her whole family bunched up at the head of the bed, trying to see BJ. I walked over to the other side of the bed and held Nina's hand.

"Oh, what a wonderful boy," Nina's mother said in her Spanish accent.

Nina smiled slightly and handed BJ to her mother. She took him and hugged him, then turned him around so Nina's father could clearly see him, and said, "Oh Joe, look at him. Isn't he beautiful?"

Nina's parents, who already had several grandchildren, passed BJ back and forth to each other for a few minutes, admiring him, while Nina's two sisters and brother spoke with her. After a while they too sat down, and each took turns holding BJ for several minutes. As he was passed around among Nina's family, Nina kept her eyes on him, closely monitoring how he was being handled, occasionally issuing cautions to them. "Be careful with him." "Support his head." "Hold him with two hands." Intermittently BJ's mouth would fall open wide, and Nina would say, "Close his mouth, please."

It was no doubt helpful for everyone in Nina's family to get to hold BJ. But by about 6:30 a.m., day had broken, and MaryAnn was preparing to move Nina up to the fifth floor. So Nina's family left, each one of them kissing Nina and BJ good-bye as they did. Her mother went last. First she kissed Nina, both of them crying. Then she held BJ one last time, closing her eyes and pressing her cheek to his. She then handed BJ back to Nina and ran out of the room, tears rolling down her face. Nina lay there for a few minutes holding BJ and forlornly wiping his brow with her hand. After a short while she fell back asleep, BJ lying on her chest. I picked the baby up and walked around the room a little more. As I was standing behind the curtain near the door, I heard a familiar voice in the hallway say, "Brad?"

It was my mother.

I peeked from behind the curtain and saw my mom and dad both standing in the doorway, both wearing expressions of eagerness and somberness. I backed up from the curtain a bit, holding BJ, and said to them, "Come on in."

They walked in together, my mom slightly in front of my dad. As she pulled back the curtain and saw BJ, his head resting on my shoulder, a look of deep hurt and sorrow fell over her face. She walked towards me, arms outstretched, her head tilted, starting to cry. I handed BJ to her as she said in a soft but expressive voice, "Oh, let me hold him, let me hold him."

She brought him to her breast, as she had long ago with me and my two brothers. She closed her eyes and patted BJ on the back, slowly rocking from side to side. I stepped back and watched with an incompatible combination of great satisfaction and deep, aching sorrow. My dad was standing next to her. She opened her eyes and turned to him, slightly extending BJ out to him, and said, "Hold him."

My dad, his eyes wet with tears, shook his head and uttered a barely audible, "No."

My heart sunk. My mom looked at him, confused, and again closed her eyes, hugging BJ even tighter than before, his limp head slightly rolling on her shoulder as she slowly twisted from side to side.

At the moment my dad refused to hold BJ, I experienced a profound sense of frustration and rejection. I felt a nausea and tightness in my stomach, similar to what I felt in Dr. Lloyd's office two days before, as he frantically searched Nina's womb for BJ's heartbeat. Although, looking back, I'm certain my father only declined to hold him at that moment out of confusion, surprise, and shock—just as I had refused to cut BJ's umbilical cord—it seemed to me, at that moment in that room, that I had failed him once again. My son was not acceptable to him. His first grandchild, the child who was to be a demonstration to my parents of my filial competence and devotion as a son, was not fit to be embraced. What I thought would be a moment of achievement for me as their youngest son—the one who had always been outshone by his two older brothers—instead had become yet another case of my failure and inferiority. I tried to resist these false feelings, but they gnawed at me.

As I stood there, watching my mom weep over BJ and my dad standing next to her, a memory from fifteen years earlier flashed before me. I was thirteen years old, heading somewhere in the car with my father. We were passing through a busy intersection near our house. There had been a serious traffic accident at the intersection just a few minutes earlier. Two mangled cars lay smoking in the road. Paramedics and firemen were working on the injured. As a police officer directing traffic in the intersection waved us through, my dad and I both turned and beheld the frightening scene. He turned back to me and yelled, "There, you see that! You see what happens when you aren't careful! Don't you ever let that happen again, mister, do you understand?"

I protested that I had nothing to do with the accident, and we spoke of it no further. But remaining with me for the rest of my adolescence and on into my adulthood was the understanding that I was to control the forces around me, that accidents and disasters could be prevented if I was responsible and careful, and that when things went wrong, it was ultimately my fault. I felt as though my father's rejection of BJ implicated me in his death. I had not met my duties as a son, husband, and father. I had not been careful enough.

My parents and I spent a few more minutes together in the quiet room. They both were clearly heartbroken at the loss, for I had never before seen such pain in their eyes. I don't think they were prepared to see BJ as he was: a fully developed, full-term baby with a face that reflected his family.

The magnitude of the loss became clear to them in the room that morning, and the combination of grief, frustration, empathy for Nina and me, and abject sorrow was plainly etched into their faces. I agreed to meet them back at my house later that day, and they left the room in silence, arm in arm.

Chapter 7

The Deepest Song of Human Desolation

*M*aryAnn had packed up a cart with our things on it to push up to the fifth floor.

"Brad," she said as she opened the blinds in the room, letting in the bracing August sun, "I'm going to get Nina ready for the move up to the fifth floor. I've put all your things on this cart, including this manila envelope, which has your pictures, footprints, and handprints, lock of hair, and some information from the hospital for you."

"Thanks," I said wearily.

She tried waking Nina up, to make it easier to transfer her to a gurney, but she was still quite drowsy. With the help of another nurse, they put Nina on a gurney, and I put BJ in the warming table (which was on wheels). The other nurse had left, and since MaryAnn was pushing Nina, I started pushing the cart with our things on it. Instantly I realized no one was pushing BJ.

"MaryAnn, wait," I said, as she was nearing the door. "What about BJ?"

"Oh." She blushed. "Sorry about that. Uh, let's leave him here, and I'll take you up to your room, and then I'll come back for him."

"I don't want to leave him here alone!" I nearly screamed, viscerally recoiling from the idea.

It seemed like a terrible thing to do, leaving him in the room all by himself, like a piece of furniture. It felt like we would be rejecting him. Besides, it didn't seem safe to me. What if someone passing by the room looked in and saw him there alone. I feared they could take him, or somehow mutilate his body.

"I'll push him myself, MaryAnn. I can do both carts at the same time."

We left the room and started down the hallway, away from the nurses' station and toward a different elevator than the one we had used to enter the maternity floor. Nina started to wake up a bit. She raised her head and said in a loud, panicked voice, "Where's BJ? Where's BJ?"

"I've got him right back here, honey," I said loudly, so she would be able to hear me.

She put her head back down on the pillow, as MaryAnn continued down the hall.

We came upon a few people in the hallway as we neared the elevator, and they could not resist peering in at BJ as we walked by. I could tell they knew something was not right with the baby, by the looks of curiosity and confusion on their faces.

We all crammed into the elevator, the four of us and our equipment, and we rode to the fifth floor. When we arrived at our room, a friendly nurse greeted us. Her name was Anna. She was short, with curly dark hair and dark skin. She and MaryAnn helped Nina into the bed. Then MaryAnn left, saying she would come back later in the morning to say good-bye to us.

Anna said to us warmly, "I just wanted to meet you and let you know you should call me if you want anything at all, okay? Just press your call button and I'll be right in."

She left, closing the door tightly behind her. Nina and I both exhaled as I picked BJ up out of his warming table and handed him to Nina. She was wide awake now, and she gazed intently into his eyes.

"He's so perfect," she said softly. "I can't get over how much he looks like you and your dad. He's your son all right, no question about that."

I took my shoes off and climbed into the bed with Nina and BJ. It was now about 7:30 a.m., and the bright summer sun streamed in through the window, gently bathing BJ's head. His blond hair shimmered.

"He looks like an angel," I said, kissing his left cheek.

"He *is* an angel," Nina said emphatically, rubbing her fingers slowly through his thin, soft hair.

"I love you, Nina," I said, turning my head toward hers and kissing her temple.

"I love you so much," she replied, with a slight smile.

"I can't believe we went through that."

"I know," Nina said, exhaling.

"Do you feel okay, honey?"

"I feel so tired, so lost and empty," Nina said, as she continued rubbing BJ's head. "I still can't believe we lost him and that we'll be going home without him. It's such a bad dream. I can't believe it."

I turned to her and kissed her cheek. She started to cry a bit as she said, "I feel like I let you down, like I did something wrong."

"Nonsense, Nina."

"But he was your boy, honey, he's your son," she continued. "You should have had him to play with, to be with."

"Nina," I said, a little irritated, "it's all right. Come on, don't say stuff like that. You did everything right. You did everything you were supposed to do. Don't say you did something wrong, okay, because you didn't. Everyone knows that. This just happened."

"But why, honey?" Nina asked, urgent. "Why did this happen, why did this happen to us. Why?"

I shook my head and squeezed her as I looked at BJ. "I have no idea why this happened, honey. No idea. I just don't know anything."

We sat there for a few minutes in silence. Nina had pulled BJ up higher on her chest, so that now our three heads were crowded together, touching. I watched as both Nina's breath and mine danced on BJ's head, slightly tussling his thin blond strands. For a moment I imagined we could breathe life into him with our love and make everything okay.

"You did so good, honey." I looked over BJ's head, into her eyes. "You were so brave, and you tried so hard. You did everything exactly right."

"You helped me too, honey, you counted for me," she said, as we both chuckled. Then she sniffled. "What are we going to do without him? It's going to seem so lonely at home."

"I don't know, honey," I said vacantly, shaking my head. "I wish we were going to have him with us."

I wanted to comfort Nina, to say something important and meaningful, but my mind was empty. The two of us lay there in silence. We knew these were sacred moments we would never have again. For about another half hour we were still and quiet, just holding BJ, passing him between us.

I wondered what he had been through in the womb, what kind of trauma he suffered. Did he suffocate, struggling for oxygen? Or did he just pass out, lose consciousness, and then never regain it? I imagined the confusion, and even fear, he may have felt, not to mention pain. How I wished I could have helped him. I recalled the huge cord and how brutal it looked. Why did God design human reproduction this way? It didn't seem like a very safe or wise plan to me. I felt an intense flash of anger at God. I became aware of how fast my heart was racing, then I took a series of deep breaths.

Nina and I continued to lie there with BJ. It was so peaceful and quiet we eventually fell asleep. I awakened, startled, fearing hours had gone by. I checked the clock on the wall. It was now about 9:00 a.m. I got out of the bed, put my shoes on, and walked around to the other side of the bed. I looked out the window at the sizzling August sun and the southern California freeway traffic in the distance. As I stared at the cars crawling on their way, I became aware that I felt uneasy. Something felt wrong.

I walked over to the foot of the bed and looked at BJ lying on top of Nina. Such a precious sight. As I stared at BJ, I noticed he looked slightly different. His fingertips and eyelids seemed redder to me, and his skin had subtly changed color, looking a little more pale, the contrast between it and the red splotches greater.

I was at that moment seized with a powerful feeling that it was somehow inappropriate, even improper, for us to stay in the room with BJ any longer. Something about it seemed wrong. I knew with a God-given certainty it was time to say good-bye to him.

I had dreaded this moment since the first few minutes after finding out we had lost him. Every cell of my body resisted the idea of letting him go. I put my face in my hands and rubbed my forehead hard, wiping the fresh perspiration back through my hair. My heart began pounding. I paced back and forth at the foot of the bed for a few minutes, trying to figure out what to tell Nina. I realized there was nothing I could tell her that was going to help her through this moment. Without even thinking about it, I realized I was talking to God. "Lord be with us, Lord help us, Lord strengthen us."

"Nina," I said in a full, robust voice, "wake up."

Nina's eyes flew open, and a look of horrible recognition flashed through them. We locked eyes for a few seconds. We both knew what we were about to have to do. Again my heartbeat quickened. I felt my mouth become dry. I walked over to

Nina and picked BJ up and held him tightly. I closed my eyes and squeezed him, again concentrating on the feeling.

"Oh, BJ, Daddy loves you sooo much," I said slowly, with my eyes still closed. I felt tears coming as I held him out in front of me and kissed his forehead.

"He's our boy, Nina," I said to her, my voice breaking as I walked around the room with him again. Nina began to cry, her torso slightly convulsing as she did.

"I love you, BJ," I whispered into his perfect little ear, as I held him tight, walking over to Nina. I handed him to her, and she took him. She began weeping loudly, her whole body bouncing up and down on the bed.

"I wish he was coming home with us, Brad, I wish we could have him!" Nina said through sobs, as she turned her head to the side, closed her eyes, and pressed her cheek against BJ's brow.

Again I was overcome by the knowledge that the time had come to say good-bye. I leaned over and kissed BJ hard, right on the top of his head. He had a clean, perfumed smell to him. I kissed Nina's damp forehead and then quickly turned around and firmly pressed the call button.

"Yes," an unfamiliar voice calmly answered.

"Send our nurse, please!" I quickly yelled into the speaker, my voice dissolving into tears, with Nina's cries crescendoing.

I lay over on top of BJ and Nina, hugging her as we both began wailing. Tears were flowing out from my eyes, cascading down my face, onto BJ and Nina. My stomach muscles were tightening with each breath.

"I love you, honey!" I screamed.

"I love you, I love you," Nina choked through tears.

About ten seconds later our nurse, Anna, rapidly knocked on the door and opened it. Immediately I forced myself up with my arms, and, still leaning over the bed, swiftly picked up BJ from under his arms, pulling him away from Nina's suddenly strong, resisting grip. As I took him her arms limply fell away, and I heard her groan from deep down within herself. I wheeled around and shouted to the nurse, "Take him! Take him now!" as I hurriedly placed him on his back in the warming table next to me, his face tilting toward me as I turned away and collapsed on top of Nina, who was whimpering in agony, covering her face with her hands. The nurse immediately grabbed the warming table and very quickly wheeled it out of the room and into the hallway, the door closing solidly behind her.

Nina and I began screaming at the top of our lungs, inarticulate, primal shouts utterly filled with unspeakable pain. It was the ancient, indescribable anguish of soul that marks the earthly parting of mother and child, father and child. It was the deepest song of human desolation. We screamed at the top of our lungs, powerless to temper our shrieks. I remember wondering what the people in the hallway and in the other rooms must be thinking about our screams, but they were beyond our control. We were being carried along a rushing river of grief, and there was nothing we could do about it.

We lay there and cried until we could not cry anymore, our bodies completely limp and weak. After nearly an hour I sighed and struggled to get up. I stood by the bedside, leaning against the wall, rubbing my eyes. Nina sat up a bit in her bed, her hollow eyes staring at her empty arms.

"Do you want anything, honey, do you want me to pour your water?" I asked slowly.

"No, I'm just, I'm not thirsty or anything. I'm just tired."

There was a small knock on the door, and MaryAnn leaned in.

"Hi there," she said tentatively, noticing our battered faces. "I'm off now, and I just wanted to say bye to you both."

She walked over to Nina and bent down and hugged her, then stood upright and held Nina's hands in her own. "You did well today, I want you to know that. I won't forget you two," she said, dabbing at her right eye.

Nina mustered a faint, exhausted smile.

"Thanks for everything, MaryAnn," I said, as she left the room without turning around.

I stood there for a minute, feeling uneasy. *Where had they put BJ?* I wondered. *What if they left him out in the hallway?* As I was trying to imagine where he was, Nina said, "Brad, why don't you go back to our house and see your parents or something. I want to try to sleep. I'm feeling tired again."

As Nina spoke, I realized something. "Honey, I have to do something about a funeral. I've got to make some kind of arrangements." I spoke haltingly, the enormity and awfulness of the task dawning on me. There was a moment of silence.

"What do you want me to do?" I asked her.

Without the slightest hesitation, she said, "Do whatever you think is best. I just, I, I just can't think about it. I can't think about it."

She rubbed her face and began rolling over to one side. I could see that she was in desperate need of sound sleep.

"Okay, honey," I said with more energy, "I'm going to go, and I'll be back here to see you early this afternoon, okay, probably in about three or four hours or so."

I walked towards her and tenderly kissed her forehead. Her eyes were closed, and she was already drifting off to sleep.

I left the room and headed toward the nurses' station, fearing I might see BJ somewhere along the way. As I reached the nurses' area, Jenny Howard came around the corner and nearly ran into me.

"Oh, Mr. Stetson, I was just going down to your room. How are you and your wife now?"

"Well, not too good, but, you know. Where's BJ right now?" I asked, with a sense of urgency.

"He's in my private office right behind the nurses' station," she said in a no-nonsense voice, making a sweeping gesture with her left arm. "I've locked the door. He's perfectly safe in there. Nobody goes in there but me. You have nothing to worry about."

"Thank you," I said, relieved, as I started down the hallway, toward the elevator. I turned behind me and looked back at Nina's door. I caught a glimpse of Dr. Lloyd walking up to the door and knocking on it. I was glad he was checking on Nina.

A few steps later I reached the elevator that would take me to the ground floor of the hospital. The doors opened and I walked in. The elevator was empty and I stood alone in the middle of it, preparing myself to start thinking about funeral arrangements and how I was going to go about making them. I was holding in my hand the manila envelope MaryAnn had given us earlier, with the pictures and information from the hospital in it. I remembered checking it earlier, in our first room, and noticing it included a listing of local mortuaries. I was about to draw the paper out of the envelope, when the elevator lurched to a stop on the fourth floor.

As the doors opened I stepped back and saw a man and woman beaming. She was in a wheelchair, holding their newborn baby. They were making that joyful trip home from the hospital with their precious gift.

I suddenly felt faint as the man pushed his wife inside the elevator. I stepped back again, leaning up against the elevator wall for support. I exhaled loudly, exhausted, as I stared blankly at the beautiful baby. Behind the mother's wheelchair was a large basket, filled with plants, flowers, a few congratulatory cards, and a red balloon, which said in big white letters, "It's a boy!"

I allowed myself to be overcome with jealousy and self-pity during the brief ride on that elevator. Here they were, going home with their precious baby boy, overjoyed and rapturously happy. All I had was a manila envelope, containing photos of my dead son. The contrast was stunning to me. *What a bizarre situation,* I thought.

I noticed a look of supreme contentment and maternal bliss on the mother's face. Her hair had just been combed, and she looked fresh and radiant. She was looking down at her baby, her eyes bright, her lips pulled taut in a deeply satisfied smile. The baby himself looked pink and healthy. His face was much fuller than BJ's, and his body looked longer. As the baby uttered a few soft cries, the mother stroked his head gently. A vision of Nina's face in an intensely pained, devastated pose flashed before me. The elevator doors opened and the family exited. I got off behind them, then quickly walked past them heading for the parking lot, trying to prepare myself for what I would have to do that morning.

CHAPTER 8

Difficult Arrangements

When I arrived home, my parents were sitting in the living room silently reading the newspaper. They both looked quite tired. They had risen very early in the morning to make the two-hour drive to the hospital. When I walked in, they both stood up. As my mother hugged me, my dad asked, "How is Nina doing?"

"Well," I said, "she's really tired. She was asleep when I left her."

"How long will she have to be in the hospital?" Mom asked.

"They didn't say. I guess whenever Dr. Lloyd lets her go home. It'll be a day or two, I suppose. Listen," I continued as we all sat down in the living room. "There's going to be a funeral. We've got to have a memorial service of some kind."

"Oh." My mom gasped, apparently surprised. "Yes," she said with a note of recognition, "you should do that. What are you going to do?"

"I really have no idea." I shook my head. "All I know is, we want to do it soon and get it over with. I need to make arrangements to have BJ cremated and try to have a service on Saturday."

"Cremated!" my mother exclaimed. She continued staring at me, with a look that said, "You've got to be kidding." I didn't answer her.

"That'll be hard to have a service on Saturday," my dad warned. "This is already Thursday morning, so you're only giving yourself forty-eight hours to make arrangements."

"Well," I said, "that's what we want to do. So I'm going to go now and look into it."

"Where will you go, dear?" my mom asked plaintively.

"I don't know. I guess I'll just start with Mission Mortuary."

This was the local mortuary in our town. I'd driven by it a thousand times, though never actually gone inside. The man who owned and managed it was the father of a girl I had known casually in high school.

I headed to the door to begin this unpleasant task when my father said softly, "Let me go with you, Brad. I'll give you a hand."

"No, that's okay, Dad, you don't need to. I can take care of it."

"I know." He touched my shoulder with his hand. "I just want to come along."

So my father and I went to Mission Mortuary to make arrangements to bury my son, his grandson. We had driven by this place so many times: on the way to baseball games, school, friends' houses, even the hardware store. What I was doing with him now felt surreal.

We parked in the lot and walked in. I was in something of a frantic and agitated state of mind. I was of course exhausted, and that fact, along with my desire to have the memorial service on Saturday, made me feel harried and rushed.

A receptionist greeted us with a plastic smile, saying in slow motion, "How can we assist you today?"

"I need to talk to somebody about funeral arrangements," I blurted.

"Okay, why don't you gentlemen just walk right down to Mr. Hempstead's office, second door on the left."

I quickly headed for the office, my dad trailing. I walked in the open door as Mr. Hempstead stood and said, "Come in, please."

This is the undertaker from central casting, I thought as I sat in front of his massive, paper-strewn redwood desk. He was thin and bald, with long, stringy gray hair ringing the bottom of his head. His face was thin and his complexion gray. His hands, neck, and forehead were creased with deep wrinkles.

My dad came in, introduced himself, and sat down.

"What is it?" Mr. Hempstead said to me in an unexpressive voice.

"Uh, well, uh," I stammered, "you see, I, uh, need to make some, some arrangements."

"Yes," Hempstead quickly said, sounding impatient with my fumbling. "When are you hoping to have a service?"

"This Saturday."

"Impossible," Hempstead said immediately, leaning back in his chair.

I began to feel panicked. He held his hands together in front of his chest, the fingertips on one hand touching the fingertips on the other hand, as he gazed at me.

"That will be impossible," Hempstead continued with authority. "I assure you, nobody in the industry can prepare a decent funeral with such short notice." He smiled a creepy smile at me. "Who is the deceased party?" he asked, his thin lips curling upward, creating a look of slight enjoyment.

I didn't want to answer his question, partly because it was hard for me to say the words "my son" in response to such a question, but also because I felt a strong dislike for this man, and in some way felt as though to mention BJ's death to him would be to cheapen it.

"It's my newborn son," I said, my voice cracking with emotion.

My father shifted uncomfortably in his seat. Hempstead looked impassively into my eyes.

My father cleared his throat and said, "What would be the earliest date you could provide a memorial service?"

"Monday," Hempstead snapped, without removing his heavy gaze from me.

I turned and looked at my father, who had what I recognized as an annoyed expression on his face. I turned back and looked at Hempstead, who was still staring at me. At that moment I just wanted to get out of that place. I knew we were not going to have anything to do with Hempstead.

"Okay," I said with a false cheeriness to my voice. I stood up.

My father stood up a little more slowly, looking at Hempstead. We were heading for the door when Hempstead leaned forward and said, "The only suggestion I can give you is to go to the office of Santiago Cemetery. They might be able to accommodate you if you're willing to settle for a public cemetery."

My father turned back to him and politely said, "Thank you."

I had heard Mr. Hempstead's suggestion, but I was already halfway down the hall, nearly running away from his office. I exited the mortuary into the August glare, quickly put my sunglasses on, and muttered, "I'm glad I never got to know his daughter any better."

"What a cold fish," my dad said.

We made the short drive to Santiago Cemetery, which was in the next city. There the cemetery office was nothing more than a shack, with a desk and some file cabinets. I walked in and was greeted by a cemetery worker, whose white uniform shirt was stitched with the name "Manuel." He got up from behind the desk and said with a broad smile, "Hello, sir, come on in."

I sat down in a metal folding chair in front of the small desk. My father came in and sat next to me. Manuel, a large Hispanic man of about fifty, smiled again and said, "How can I help you folks?"

"Well," I said, feeling more comfortable than before, "I have to make some arrangements for a memorial service."

"Okay," Manuel said, getting up from behind the desk and walking over to one of the filing cabinets. "I'm not the manager here; I just supervise the cemetery workers. You'll need to talk with Tom Cunningham, the manager. But you can get started by filling these forms out, and I can show you around the grounds."

I filled out the papers in silence as my dad sat next to me. I was trying to think of nothing except the forms in front of me. I did not want to let my mind wander, knowing that I would break down if I thought about what I had just been through. After I finished the paperwork, the three of us went outside, and Manuel walked us around some of the cemetery. When I told him I would be cremating, he took me to a small but nice "urn garden," reserved only for cremated remains. I found a shady plot in front of a giant old pine tree and told Manuel that was what I wanted.

"Are you sure, Brad?" my dad asked, sounding surprised at my decisiveness. I nodded.

Santiago Cemetery didn't handle cremations itself, so we drove over to the Green Family Mortuary nearby. A nice young man there, no more than twenty-two years old, helped us. His name was Phillip Salmon. As I looked at his red hair, pink skin, and pink lips, it occurred to me he even looked salmon-like. I nearly said something to my dad about it, but thought that I was just getting punchy from the stress and lack of sleep.

Phillip was extremely helpful. At one point he said earnestly, "I want to call the hospital while you're here, because to have the cremation done for you by Saturday, I need to pick the body up today. Who should I call out there, do you know?"

I turned and looked at my father, and he looked at me, sharing my blank expression. As Phillip dialed the general hospital number, Jenny Howard's name came to my mind. I recalled her telling me BJ was safe in her office, and that no one could get to him but her. I told him to ask for her, and a few minutes later I heard him introduce himself to her over the phone. His conversation with her was short. He then hung up the phone and said, "Well, I think we're all set then. What time are you having the service and where?"

Remembering the majestic pine tree next to BJ's plot and the peacefulness of that old cemetery, I said to Phillip, "We'd like to just have a brief graveside service at, say, 1:00 p.m., on Saturday, right at Santiago Cemetery. Do you think that would be all right?"

Phillip studiously took notes as I spoke, then asked, "Will you need a minister or rabbi or someone, or do you have somebody?"

"We've already got somebody," I said, realizing I would have to call our pastor, Ed, and ask him to conduct the small service. I knew he would do it. I was glad I had a pastor to turn to for such a momentous and significant task and would not have to go through the awkward inconvenience of having to hire someone I did not know.

"Well, that will do it. I'll call the cemetery, make sure 1:00 p.m. Saturday works for them, and we're set." I gave him my credit card, and he charged the bill on it.

On the way home in the car, my dad leaned over and lightly put his arm around me. "You handled all that very well, Brad," he said.

I pretended not to notice his compliment. We rode on in silence, but I could tell he wanted to say something more. He shifted in his seat restlessly for a few minutes, then cleared his throat. "This whole thing must have been awful for you and Nina." He paused a bit. "I can't imagine what it must have been like."

"Yes," I said quietly.

"Well, I just want you to know Mom and I both think you've handled everything very well, and we hope it all works out for the best."

I felt extremely proud as he spoke, but I tried to resist smiling. "Well," I said, trying to think of something appropriate to say, "thank you. And thanks for coming with me to do this. I appreciate it."

"Well, you didn't need my help. You seem quite capable yourself."

Then, after a pause, he said, his voice slightly choking, "I'm proud of you."

I felt tears well up in my eyes, but I suppressed them. We arrived home a few moments later.

That conversation with my father was very important to me, even as simple and stilted as it was. Although he didn't express any deeply profound sentiment, he communicated to me, as best he could, his respect for me, not just as his son, but as a man. It marked in my mind my father's acceptance of me as a competent man, as someone who, like him, was able to handle difficult situations and, in the midst of them, be responsible and maintain self-control. Also, I began to feel that he clearly understood the impossibility of my preventing BJ's stillbirth from happening. He grasped the helplessness I felt, and I sensed his absolution.

When we walked into the house, my mom was talking on the phone to her longtime friend Connie. I could tell she had been crying. She hung up shortly after we came in, and the three of us went to the living room and sat down again.

"How did it go?" my mom said with a concerned look on her face.

"Fine," I said, rubbing my eyes. "The service is 1:00 p.m. on Saturday at Santiago Cemetery, graveside. It's going to be really short, like fifteen minutes or so. I don't think Nina and I are going to be up for anything more than that."

"That's fine," my dad said reassuringly.

"I've got to go back to the hospital and see Nina," I said. "You can just stay here if you like."

"Go ahead, dear," my mom said sympathetically. "We'll stop by here again later tonight. If you're here, maybe we'll see you then."

When I saw Nina about a half hour later she was awake and having a small bowl of soup. I was surprised at how well she looked. Her eyes were more alert, and she had more energy than she had just a few hours earlier.

"Hi, honey," I said, walking in briskly.

"Hi, how did it go?"

"The memorial service will be at 1:00 p.m. on Saturday."

"Oh, good," she said with a relieved sigh. "I was hoping we could do it soon like that."

We talked about what Dr. Lloyd said at his visit and what she would do the rest of her time in the hospital. She wanted very much to get out of there, but she, like me, was dreading the funeral. As she told me about how much she wanted to get the funeral over with, I remembered that a friend of mine in college whose father had died told me that the hardest time for him was the time between finding out about the death of his dad and the actual funeral service.

Nina said Dr. Lloyd had told her she could go home tomorrow morning if she seemed up to it. She said she wanted to very much and asked me to call her family and a few of her close friends, informing them of the service, and asking them to come to it. After kissing her and sitting with her for a few more minutes, I went back home and made the phone calls.

As I was going back out to the hospital in the evening to see Nina, it occurred to me that the memorial service should seem like a memorial service, not just a bunch of people standing around at the cemetery for a few minutes. It should clearly acknowledge the reality of BJ's life and loss. I trusted Pastor Ed and Santiago Cemetery to do their parts toward that end, but I felt like I should do something as well. My mind wandered through ideas: a program, a flier, some kind of printed announcement to give people. Any one of those things would be fine, but I was running out of energy to do them, plus I was concerned about having them ready by Saturday. So I simply decided to stop at a florist near our house and order some kind of flower arrangement.

I walked into the busy store and wandered around, looking at displays. I was feeling extremely sad. *We should be placing BJ in his crib in his bedroom at home*, I thought, *not in the ground*. After several minutes a middle-aged woman who seemed like the manager came to me and said, "What can I help you with?"

"Uh, I need to, I need to get a large flower arrangement."

"Sure," the rotund woman said. She was about my height, 5'10", with red hair and freckles, and she seemed very friendly. "What's the occasion?"

I paused for a while, trying to think of a way to avoid telling her, because I sensed I was near being overcome with tears yet again. Finally, I mumbled, looking at the ground, "A funeral."

"Oh," she said, her voice dipping. "Well, who's it for?"

The tears started coming. I looked up and said quickly, "My son was stillborn."

The woman looked shocked for a moment, then a look of deep empathy settled on her face.

"Oh, oh, I'm so sorry," she said, taking a step toward me.

I wiped my face again, trying to suppress the tears, but they kept coming. They were beyond my control. The woman could see I was grief-stricken, and she took another step toward me and put her large arms around me.

That act of compassion from this stranger, along with my exhaustion and pain, led me to even deeper weeping. I squeezed her hard and began sobbing uncontrollably into her shoulder, dampening her T-shirt.

"Oh, that's okay, go ahead, go ahead," she soothed.

By this time people in the store had started staring. The employees had stopped their work behind the counter, and people were curiously walking past us. I continued crying into the woman's shoulder for a few minutes. Finally I took a step back and tried to regain composure.

"Was that your first baby?" the woman asked, sounding hopeful my answer would be no.

"Yes," I said, gulping air.

"Oh," she said again, this time a little more intensely, and with a look of disappointment. "Come over here and sit down, dear, take a rest for a minute."

She led me over to a chair behind the counter. After several more minutes I pulled myself together, while bustling workers uneasily moved around me. The manager asked me my son's name, then wrote "BJ" in large cursive letters on a sheet of poster board. She showed it to me and said they would deliver it along with the flower arrangement to the cemetery. I thanked her for her help and left the store, feeling even more drained than when I arrived an hour earlier.

I went straight to the hospital. Walking the now familiar halls, I would occasionally see new mothers with their babies leaving the hospital to go home. I had learned not to look closely at such scenes. The pain was too sharp. So I walked briskly through the halls, concentrating on keeping my eyes focused straight ahead of me on the ground.

When I walked into Nina's room, she was napping. I sat next to her bed for a long time, holding her hand while she slept, watching the television with the sound muted. After about an hour or so Nina woke up.

When she did, I leaned over and kissed her.

"I missed you," she said with a small smile.

"I missed you too. Are you doing all right?"

"Yeah," she said, her eyes drifting around the room.

"I can't wait for tomorrow though; I want to get out of here. Jenny Howard came by and said I'll be going home as soon as Dr. Lloyd sees me in the morning. She said he's coming about 9:00 a.m."

"Good," I said, relieved.

I was hoping I could take Nina out of the hospital before it became too busy, wanting to avoid the frightening sight of new mothers and their babies.

We sat and talked about the last few days and what a trauma they had been. We told each other over and over how perfect BJ was and how much he looked like my father and me.

"You know, honey, I was thinking," Nina said slowly, "in one way we were lucky. It would have been so much harder had we gone to the hospital expecting to have BJ be born alive, and then have him be stillborn. I think we were lucky we knew ahead of time."

"Yes," I said, stroking her forehead.

"Or if he had been born alive, and we had held him, and then he died shortly afterward."

"I know, honey," I said, standing up. "If he had died of cancer as a toddler, been hit by a car at age seven, or shot by a gang in high school, all of those things would have been awful. It hurts beyond words, no matter how or when you lose your child. It's too much to imagine."

"You have the pictures MaryAnn took, right, Brad?"

"They're at home, honey. I put them right on the kitchen counter."

"Good," she said. "I want to save those forever."

I leaned over and kissed her on the lips as her eyes welled with tears. We didn't say anything for a long time. We just held hands, watched television, and napped off and on. Later that night Nina fell asleep, and I took the opportunity to slip out of her room and head home, walking alone again through the silent, barren hospital hallways.

As I walked, I wondered about the next few days. Although there was still lurking in me an unresolved—even unacknowledged—anger at God, I knew that he was going to be with us in the next few days, and on into the future. Like a son who fights with his father but knows that if he gets in trouble and needs his father, his father will help him even though they just had a fight, so it was, I felt, with God and me. He would not allow my misplaced anger at him to isolate or harm me. He would be in my tomorrows even if tomorrow I would not consciously be in him.

CHAPTER 9

A Funeral of Unbearable Sadness

*T*he next morning I arrived at Nina's room just as Dr. Lloyd was leaving.

"She's ready to go, Brad. I'll need to see her back in my office in six weeks though, for a postpartum check. I've given her a prescription for some pills that will dry up her milk, so hopefully she won't feel too uncomfortable."

"Okay, thanks, Dr. Lloyd. I'll talk with you later."

He looked at me and nodded. Patting my shoulder, he said, "Good luck."

I walked in and Nina was standing by her bed, packing her bag.

"Do you feel ready to go, honey?"

"Absolutely. I want to get out of here. I want to get back home."

A nurse came with a wheelchair for Nina. On the way out I walked in front of Nina like a blocker, hoping to distract her if we ran into a mother leaving. We got to the door. Nina and the nurse waited while I pulled our car around. Nina got in, along with a few flowers we'd been sent, and then we drove away from the hospital. As we passed the small building next to the hospital where we'd had our Lamaze classes, Nina kept her gaze forward.

We spent that day at home relaxing. Nina, who always had a cleaning compulsion, did as much as she felt she could, with me every few minutes asking her to stop and take it easy on herself. She went to bed early that night as I lay on the couch channel surfing. About midnight, I heard her call me. I ran upstairs to find her sitting up in bed, the room brightly lit.

"Brad," she said softly. I could tell she had been crying. "Let's look at our pictures of BJ."

Without saying anything I went back downstairs and picked up the envelope which had the pictures inside it. Back upstairs, I sat down next to her on the bed. We pulled all five of the pictures out of the envelope, plus the lock of hair and the sheet with BJ's footprints and handprints on it. We studied the footprints and handprints.

"His feet are so little, Brad," Nina said, gazing at the prints. Then we stared at each picture carefully.

"Look at his face, honey. He has such a serious look on his face, like you. He got your nerves. I hoped he wouldn't have been uptight, like you."

"He would have been a good boy, honey," I said, rubbing her back. "He would have been a good little boy."

"I can't get over that blond hair." Nina touched the image of the hair on the picture. She picked up the small lock of blond hair, which was bound together with a rubber band, and rubbed the soft golden strands against her cheek.

Nina said wistfully, "I wish so much he was with us now. I wish he was always going to be with us."

I put my arm around her as she cried slightly, turning her head into my chest.

"We'll always have him, honey," I said firmly. "He will always be our son, and we'll always remember him. He is always going to be a part of our lives. That is something that will never change."

I recalled reading a story attributed to Henry Ward Beecher in the devotional classic *Streams in the Desert*. Beecher said he was sitting on a hillside one day, watching a storm pass through a valley. The dark clouds settled over the land, obscuring it, and the thunder seemed to batter it. Certainly, he thought, the tender flowers of the valley will be trampled and carried away in the torrent of rain dropped by this storm. After some time, the wind and rain subsided, the skies calmed, and the storm moved on. Beecher imagined himself returning to that same hillside the next day and asking the grass of the valley, "Where is that intense storm and all its terrible darkness?" He wrote that the grass would have said, "Part of it is in me." So too, the beautiful daisy would have answered that question, "Part of it is in me." And all of the other flowers of the valley, and all the other trees and plants that live there, would have similarly answered, "Part of the storm has produced the radiance you see in me today." Beecher goes on to say, "Storms bring blessings, and rich fruit will be harvested later." The losses we suffer in our lives and the sorrow they bring nourish our humanity; they enlarge our souls and yield a richer color to our lives. They are part of the new person we become.

So, too, I hoped that BJ's life and the sustained suffering we would experience because of his death would be absorbed into our lives and cause us to grow. He would never leave us, and we would never go on with our lives apart from his touch.

Nina handed me the pictures, prints, and hair, and I meticulously put them back in the envelope and sealed it. She sat there in silence as I put the envelope away. Again I remembered a poem by Henry Sutton I'd read in *Streams in the Desert.* I spoke it aloud:

> *"The flowers live by the tears that fall*
> *From the sad face of the skies;*
> *And life would have no joys at all,*
> *Were there no watery eyes.*
> *Love the sorrow, for grief will bring*
> *Its own reward in later years;*
> *The rainbow! See how fair a thing*
> *God has built from tears."*

Nina closed her eyes and wept softly as I lay next to her holding her hand. Although those words were a beautiful encouragement, the blanket of sadness still covered us so fully we could not fully appreciate them.

We both slept late the next morning and woke up at about 10:30. As I got dressed, I still felt somewhat numb. A lingering disbelief hung over me.

Nina and I drove to the cemetery in silence, getting there about twenty-five minutes early. As we drove up to the office, I saw Manuel mowing a lawn. We exchanged waves of recognition and he smiled at me as I parked near the office, a ways from BJ's plot. From that distance, though, I could see that four chairs were set up at the grave site, and the flowers from the florist had arrived and were in place.

As Nina and I walked over to the office, a stout, bespectacled man in a suit came out the door and greeted us.

"Mr. Stetson, I'm Tom Cunningham."

He gave me a firm handshake and met my eyes with a warm look.

"This is my wife, Nina," I said, motioning to Nina, who was standing next to me.

"I'm sorry about your loss," he said, looking at her with patent sincerity, even though he must have said those words a thousand times. "The Green Family Mortuary delivered the remains this morning. They're locked in my office," he said quietly as we walked toward the plot. "I'll bring them over just before you start."

I nodded my head and Nina sniffled.

Tom turned back to his office, and Nina and I walked alone the rest of the way over to the site. There was no one there yet. The flower arrangement was set up next to the grave, and attached to it was the poster-board sign the florist had made. In big blue letters it said, "BJ."

I showed the plot to Nina. It was a small hole, about two feet by three feet in the ground, several feet deep. I shuddered involuntarily as I looked into its black darkness. Even though it was a brightly lit day, the hole in the earth seemed as ebony as a moonless night. It seemed foreboding, and I felt physically ill—my stomach churned—as I looked at it. I turned away.

Nina went to one of the chairs on the lawn, just behind the flowers, in the shade of that large pine tree. She sat limply in the chair, her head downcast, her hands at her sides. I walked around the urn garden. The freshly cut grass yielded its signature scent, and I thought of baseball and all the times I had played the great game amidst such a smell, and how exuberant it made me feel. I felt an odd dissonance now, experiencing the odor of freshly mowed lawn—a smell that was for me full of life and vitality—while wearing such heavy grief and complete sadness.

The urn garden was nearly empty except for the grave of someone named Ernesto Lopez Jr., who had died at age thirty-five, and Frank Withers, who had also died at that age. There was also a tablet for someone named DeAnn K. Frost, who was described as "Beloved Mother, Wife, Daughter." She had been born in 1965, and she died in March of this year. My sadness spiked as I calculated her age. She was only twenty-six when she died. What agony her children must feel, I thought. And her husband. I looked out over the acres and acres of tombstones and tablets, imagining all the sorrow and sadness that lay behind each one.

I walked over to Nina and stood behind her, putting my hands on her shoulders and gently rubbing them. A tear trickled down my cheek as I realized that our pregnancy, which had been the center of our lives for nearly nine months, the polestar of all our hopes and plans, was ending in a cemetery, this place of deepest human sadness and ultimate loss. I silently shook my head in wonderment.

As I was standing there, I saw familiar cars arriving. One by one, they came: my parents, Nina's parents, Pastor Ed and his wife Carla, my brothers and their wives, Nina's two sisters and their husbands, her brother and his wife, Nina's friend Peggy, and a couple other close friends of hers with their husbands. They all wore somber expressions and kept their eyes focused on the ground ahead of them as they walked, weaving their way among the headstones and tablets. As they reached the urn garden, they quietly stood behind the four chairs, one of which was occupied by Nina. There were a few handshakes and hugs, but mostly silence.

I noticed my brother Stan's wife standing apart from the group, looking away from everyone, surveying the cemetery. I knew her to be a very unemotional person, always calm and personally reserved. As she turned slightly back toward the rest of us, I could see she was freely crying, her eyes red and puffy. She wiped them, not seeing me, and I turned away, understanding clearly from her reaction the unbearable sadness of this moment for everyone. Indeed, there was a thick canopy of mourning that hung over the gathering at BJ's graveside, an homage to the preciousness of his life and the innocent, unspoiled beauty and hopefulness we see in babies.

Nina motioned to her mother, who came and sat next to her and put her right arm around her. They wept together for a moment, as sniffles rippled through the gathering. I then sat next to Nina, with my left arm around her. As I sat down, she began crying more intensely. There was one more empty chair. I turned and saw my mother standing behind it, wiping a tear from her eye.

"Mom," I said, motioning to the open chair. She sat to my right. The guests clustered in, still standing behind us. Then Pastor Ed stepped to the front.

As I looked at his face carefully, I realized he looked unlike I had ever seen him before. He was an avuncular man of about age fifty, with curly brown hair. Normally he was a very easygoing and even jocular person, with an expressive face that punctuated his statements. His glasses filled up his thin face, and his deep brown eyes always had an inviting, warm look to them. But now, his brow was furrowed with concern and his jaw set in a sort of tight, brooding form. He looked profoundly serious.

As Ed positioned himself before the crowd of about twenty people, Tom Cunningham, whom I hadn't even noticed standing nearby, placed BJ's ashes in the hole in the ground. They were contained in a compact, plain white box, about the size of a small shoe box. As he bent down, he held it with two hands, knowing that what it contained was very valuable. As I looked at the box and watched Tom stick it down into the black hole, his arms disappearing just past his elbows, I tossed my head back and writhed in pain, tears bubbling up in my eyes and sliding down my cheeks. The finality of BJ's loss penetrated me, like a sword slicing through my belly. Those were my son's ashes, the remnants of his body, being laid deep into the cold dirt. I wanted to scream, "Stop! Stop!"

As Tom stepped away from the hole, Nina slumped over into me, her body slightly shaking as she wept. Tom turned and walked away. Pastor Ed cleared his throat and began speaking.

"Thank you, everyone, for coming. I've been asked just to say a few words; it won't be long."

It was August 17 in Southern California, and the sun, which had been shielded by clouds, now brutally beat down upon us. Ed was squinting as he spoke, and the glare forced Nina and me to look down at the ground just behind him, where BJ's ashes were about to be covered by the earth.

"We know that death is an enemy, and a mighty cruel one at that," Ed said. "It can take what it is least entitled to and trespass where it ought never be. Today, we're here to express our love for Nina and Brad, our support for them, and our awareness that the loss of their son is a tragic invasion of their lives by that rude enemy."

I shifted in my seat uncomfortably as Ed spoke, the unbearable sadness of the moment and my heavy grief pressing down on me. Nina kept her head down, softly crying the whole time.

Pastor Ed read the Bible story from 2 Samuel 12 of King David's child, whom David had conceived illicitly with Bathsheba. Shortly after birth the child became ill, and seven days later he died. David, upon hearing the child had died, was not as grieved and stricken as his servants had expected him to be. He noticed their surprise and told them simply, "While the child was still alive, I fasted and wept. I thought, 'Who knows? The Lord may be gracious to me and let the child live.' But now that he is dead, why should I fast? Can

I bring him back again? I will go to him, but he will not return to me" (2 Samuel 12:22–23).

"That story," Ed said, looking at Nina and me, "is a promise to those like you who've lost a baby. It is a promise that you will see your precious one again, after death, in heaven. Brad and Nina, that promise is for you now. I want you to know you'll see BJ again, you'll hold him in heaven, and all your tears will be wiped away. You have that promise from God's Word. Do not doubt it."

Nina was now crying loudly, her anguished voice echoing among the tombs. I tightened my squeeze around her and curled my toes in my shoes, trying to keep from bawling.

Ed continued, now speaking a little more rapidly. "God knows the pain you are feeling today, Brad and Nina. He lost a Son once, a Son who, like BJ, was an only Son. But to let us know the true purpose of our lives, and to let us know he had conquered that most horrible of enemies, God raised his Son back to life, to relationship with him. So it is for you two, that your son, though his body died, yet lives, and you will always have a special relationship with him. He was, as much as we might wish otherwise, born into God's kingdom, rather than this mortal earth. We do not know why, but we know God is good, and his love for each of us far surpasses what we can know and understand. That is a belief that will be a comfort to you, Brad and Nina, and one which you must never forget.

"But I want to warn you now," he went on, "you're in for a tough road. You will grieve. You will cry. You will scream. You will yell. Your anger will flare and your frustration fire. But do not allow yourself to sink into a pit of despair. Reach out to your friends and family. Talk to others, let them know how you feel. As painful as it might be, talk about BJ to people. Even in your sadness celebrate his life, for it was a life ordained by God."

After a long pause, Ed said softly, "Cling to one another, everyone, for your love and friendship is the balm that eases the pains of life, the salve that cools the sting of loss."

Then he asked everyone to hold hands as he prayed. "God, bless and comfort Brad and Nina and their families and friends. Let them know you are watching over them, and that your love for them is unwavering and unfaltering. May the weeks, months, and years to come see them grow closer to you and one another, and may your wise hand graciously rest upon them. In your Son's name, amen."

After he finished speaking Ed just stood there, looking at the guests. Nina and I sat in our chairs, waiting for something to happen. Ed's sermon went so quickly that I wondered if he was through. I looked around and realized nobody knew what to do. So I stood up, took a large step forward, and shook Ed's hand, saying, "Thank you."

I then turned around and reached my hand out to Nina. She put her hand in mine, and I pulled her out of her chair. She was so weak and limp, I nearly had to support all her weight as we walked away, arm in arm, without looking back.

My mind wandered back to a memory from my childhood. My father had taken our whole family to see the science fiction movie *Andromeda Strain,* about a deadly virus that wipes out an entire town. I was only a small child at the time, but I recall standing outside the theater, waiting for the movie, gazing at the poster advertising the film. My two older brothers were standing next to me. The poster featured an aerial photo of the devastated town, its stricken inhabitants lying dead. Among them I could make out a dog, what looked like a German shepherd, my favorite breed. As my brothers and I looked at this poster, I said to them, to reassure myself, "The dog is not really dead."

Brian and Stan, sensing an opportunity to tease their fragile younger brother, could not resist.

"Yes, he is, Brad," they said in unison, with the unique delight older brothers take in scaring their little brothers.

"No, he's not, he's just sleeping or pretending," I said, with a hint of desperation.

"No, Brad," one of them insisted as the other tried to keep from laughing. "The dog is dead. He's not asleep or pretending. See, he's lying like that because he's really dead."

We went on and on, back and forth, until my two brothers had successfully reduced me to tears, convincing me that the dog was actually dead. My cries attracted the attention of my parents, who pulled my brothers off of me.

As I walked with Nina across the cemetery, I felt again the same fear and torment I had felt as a small child staring at that movie poster. I wanted BJ to be alive, I wanted BJ to be alive, I didn't want this to be happening, I didn't want to finally acknowledge that he was dead. It must not be happening, this annihilation of hope. But I knew—just as I had sadly and reluctantly concluded about that dog on the movie poster—that BJ was dead. He had died and his funeral was now over. It had all genuinely happened.

When we got home, everyone from the memorial service had already started arriving. Nina busied herself by cleaning the kitchen and setting plates and silverware out, but her sisters made her stop. I walked in after her. My oldest brother Brian was standing by the door. When he saw me walk in he hugged me without saying anything. It was a tight bear hug, which lasted for about two minutes. One by one, the other men who were there, all of whom I knew at least in passing, came up to me and shook my hand. They were firm handshakes, accompanied by averted glances and inarticulate, staccato condolences, like "Sorry, man," or "Hang in there," and "Take care."

The people milled around for nearly two hours, spontaneously forming little groups, talking in hushed tones like some kind of sedate cocktail party. I sat on the couch next to Nina. We both said very little. Periodically people would come and sit near us, usually women, and talk about our house, the weather, or other pedestrian topics. Occasionally someone would mention Javert, our basset hound, who was lying next to us on the couch, lost in one of his deep sleeps. Nina's mother spent most of the time in the kitchen, trying to keep busy. She was crying nearly the whole time. Now and then my mother would go to her, and the two grandmothers would share a moment of painful loss.

The overriding sense at this gathering was one of "Now what?" Nobody knew what to say to us, the grieving couple. No one there had experienced the death of a child, and the profundity of the loss was an intimidating thing to try to address. There was an elephant in this room—our grief—and no one, especially Nina and I, knew what to do with it. But this may well have been for the best, because ultimately such tragedies cannot be explained in a single conversation or moment of condolence. Nobody, finally, would be able to bring Nina and me to grips with our loss. We ourselves needed to lean on God's love. We would have to walk the path to our emotional resolution ourselves, unaccompanied by any magic mantras or miracle pills. We would be helped by the Lord and by our friends, but as Nina and I sat there together like two scared children, holding hands, looking and feeling dazed and stunned by the events of the last five days, I think we each, in our own way, knew that our journey to a "new normal" would be an arduous one.

I began to wish that people would leave, so that Nina and I could be alone. Finally, couple by couple, people started to leave, perhaps sensing my growing discomfort. Ed and Carla were standing near the door, and as each pair left, Ed thanked them for coming. Then they too left, leaving just our families.

"We're going to go now, dear," my mom said, kissing my forehead.

"Brad, we're leaving," my dad echoed, his voice tinged with sorrow. "We'll call you tomorrow. Take care of Nina."

I hugged them both and said good-bye. Their somberness and pain depressed me. I felt, in a distant but uneasy way, that I had failed again and was the source of their heartbreak. As I watched them walk out to the car, hand in hand, I felt a deep, powerful love for them. They had accomplished so much in their lives, done so much for their children, been such fine parents. They deserved more than what happened. They deserved to enjoy the unique happiness and satisfaction of grandchildren.

I turned around and saw my two older brothers and their wives preparing to leave. I felt a sudden flash of anger toward them. Why hadn't they had children by now? Then maybe this wouldn't have happened. My parents would be happy grandparents, we might not have conceived BJ when we did, and then none of this hellish scenario would have played.

I took a deep breath, and my moment of anger subsided.

That's wrong of me, that's not fair of me, I thought. *They know when and if they should try to have children. I don't know the circumstances of their lives, I don't know God's plan for them. Anyway, for all I know, they may have been trying to have children and just not been successful.*

Each of my brothers walked over to me and shook my hand, adding a brief hug.

"Take it easy, okay?" Stan said, placing his hand on my shoulder. "Call me if you want me to pick up Javert, if you want to go out of town or something."

"Thanks."

Brian gave me another strong hug, said good-bye, then left. Nina's sisters were sitting on the couch with Nina, asking her how they could help. She said she would call them for help when she needed it, which meant she didn't want any help. Then they left, along with her parents, leaving Nina and me alone in the living room.

I went over to the couch where she was still sitting and sat down, exhaling heavily as I dropped into the comfortable cushions.

"You did so well, honey," I said, touching her leg.

She lay down and rested her head on my lap.

"I feel so empty, so miserable," Nina said in a low voice, starting to cry once again. "I was supposed to be a mommy. I was supposed to have a baby to take care of. I was supposed to be a mommy."

Her familiar sobs were vigorous and loud. Javert lifted his head and looked at her as the couch shook from Nina's cries.

"I know, honey, I know you were," I said, running my hand through her hair.

She continued to cry as I sat there at a loss for words. My mind ran through all that had happened since Tuesday. There was still a numbness within me. I remembered Mark Twain, on learning of the sudden death of his twenty-four-year-old daughter, wrote, "It is one of the mysteries of our nature that a man, all unprepared, can receive a thunderstroke like that and live."

A thunderstroke. That's how it felt, as though we had been hit by lightning. In one moment, our lives had been placed on a course completely different from what we had planned. Now, as we sat quietly together in our still house, we knew we would have no choice but to traverse that way of loss, both as individuals and as a couple. How would we do it? I wondered. Again I thought of Mark Twain. He once said that losing a loved one is like having your house burn down: it takes years to realize all that you have lost.

I understood then, with strange certainty and simple clarity, that it would take time, a lot of time, for Nina and me to fully come to grips with the stillbirth of our treasured son, whose life—like ours—would endure. We would not wake up one day and be "recovered," as though it had never happened. There would be no "getting over it." But we could learn to live with this loss and gradually be brought to a place of inner peace by the Prince of Peace himself. There was a "new normal" for which we could aspire.

Chapter 10

Return to the World

The next few days were slow. Nina and I purposely didn't do much, except be at home. On Tuesday a salesman from a marker company came by, and we selected a tablet for BJ's grave. Nina picked it. It was reddish-brown in color with white lettering. Nina had asked me to decide what the tablet should read, so since the time of the funeral, I had carefully thought about it. I told her what I had decided before the salesman came. She said she liked it, so while he was sitting with us in our living room, I carefully wrote it down on a three-by-five index card and gave it to him. The inscription we wanted said:

Bradley John Stetson
"BJ"
Born into God's Kingdom
August 15, 1991

As that first week after the funeral wore on, I persistently felt that strange feeling of disorientation and nausea I had felt all the previous week. Each day I would go to visit BJ's grave and just stand there in front of it, staring at the small rectangle of lawn that had been placed over the grave. Nina went with me the first couple of times, but I could tell she didn't really want to be there. At least not every day.

She started cleaning the house each day, scrubbing where she had already scrubbed, vacuuming where she had already vacuumed. She had always been a zealous house-cleaner, and now the activity seemed to be a way of focusing her energy. After a few days of that, she began to throw herself into her work as a kindergarten teacher. She was taking the first week after the funeral off, but since she taught at a year-round school, she was going to go back to work the following week. She started cutting out letters, making pictures, gathering pictures to laminate, and generally working full time at preparing to teach kindergarten again.

At the end of the week, I approached her as she sat at a table cutting and pasting pictures. "Nina, why are you working so hard? Why don't you take it easy?"

"Because," she said, tracing a gingerbread man, "this keeps me busy. I think I'm going to spend a little more time at work now, at least for a while."

Then, pausing and looking up at me with a look of deep pain, she said softly, "It just hurts too much to be here."

Tears began gathering in her eyes as she continued, "I think of BJ and you, and how much we wanted him, and it makes me so sad I don't know what to do."

She put her pen down and brought her hands to her face, catching the tears as they flowed. I kissed her head, then pulled a chair over and said, "I know, Nina. I feel like that too."

"I should have been a mommy, Brad!" she shouted through tears, with a mix of anger, confusion, and sadness. "I was supposed to be a mommy!"

I hugged her as she cried vigorously, and I tried to imagine how she must feel, having carried this baby for nine months, felt him inside of her, felt his life growing and his body moving, only to have him die inside of her. She had formed the deepest human connection possible for a woman—mother to child—and yet, without warning, this great bond had been doomed to incompleteness. It had not been severed, nor could it ever fully be. Indeed, it was our still strong attachment to BJ that dictated our pain, since our relationship to him would not play out through the years as we had always planned and assumed it would. The momentum of our love for him threw us forward into a wall of grief, just as passengers in a speeding car are dangerously hurtled forward when their car collides with an immovable object. By experiencing the death of her baby just when he was poised to be born, Nina's soul had been ruptured, and this was an experience of pain and sorrow so intimate, so ineffably personal, it could never be fully shared by another human being. I realized I couldn't genuinely feel what she felt, or experience all that she experienced. There would be a wall of sorts between us. We would, unavoidably, experience the grief of stillbirth separately as well as together. It would not be possible to fully know what the other was feeling.

"You did everything you were supposed to do, honey," I said, squeezing her. "You were a perfect mother to BJ. You were his mother for nine months, and"—I stopped, my voice cracking with emotion—"he loved you."

We sat together and cried for some time, feeling again the emptiness and indescribably excruciating grief with which we were becoming familiar.

As Nina went back to her students—most of whom were from poor, Hispanic immigrant families—I returned to school myself. I was a graduate student at USC, completing a degree in social ethics. This school year I was scheduled to teach a writing class for freshmen, and I had to attend an orientation week in preparation for the class.

The night before orientation, I received a phone call from the woman—another graduate student—who was supervising the orientation. "This is Patty from the freshman writing program," she said. "I just wanted to remind you that tomorrow is the first day of our orientation class. You will be coming, won't you?"

"Uh, yeah, I'm planning on coming," I said, knowing I had to go, but not wanting to commute the fifty miles every day to the school.

"You sound tired," she said kiddingly, "have you been working hard this summer?"

"Well, no, I, uh, I just haven't got a lot of sleep lately."

"Oh, how come?" she asked innocently.

This was the first time I had been put in the position of either telling someone what had happened or avoiding the subject. Part of me wanted to avoid the subject, for a number of reasons: I knew I would cry if I talked about it, making for an awkward situation with the other person. Also, it was an intensely private event, and I was reluctant to be open about it to people who were not close friends. But on the other hand, I had an overriding feeling that to avoid the subject was to deny BJ, to deny we had him, to deny his life and all that it meant to us. I desperately didn't want to do that.

So, in answer to Patty's question, I said, stumbling, "Well, uh, my wife and I had a baby a few days ago, and—"

Before I could finish, Patty exclaimed, "Oh, congratulations! That's great! Well, you won't be getting any sleep for a while then, huh?"

"Well, actually, he, uh, he was stillborn." My voice cracked noticeably as I finished my sentence.

After a second of shocked silence, Patty gasped, "Oh, I'm sorry!"

"It's okay," I said quickly, knowing she regretted saying what she had, even though it was completely natural. She had no idea what had happened to us.

"Well, I'm sorry," she said, still flustered. "How's your wife?"

I paused.

"Not well," I said flatly.

The conversation quickly drew to a close, but there would be many more like that, for both Nina and me. In particular, I remember people frequently asking me about my wife, which I appreciated, but rarely asking me how I was doing. People first thought of our son's mother when they heard we had lost him, but of course, I was stricken as well.

Although I was usually reticent to talk about our experience, I found myself sometimes yearning to hear people acknowledge the fact that I had been a father, that I had lost my son, and that I was feeling the piercing sting of that pain. Even a simple recognition along those lines always encouraged me.

Of course, especially those first few months, many of my conversations never even reached the point where someone could openly sympathize with me, as I was incapable of mentioning the event without choking up and crying. Only in the language of tears could I refer to my stillborn son, and to be confronted with a crying man was confusing to many people, who then didn't know whether to try to talk to me or leave me alone.

Such was the case when later that same night a friend of mine from graduate school, who was also attending this orientation, called to ask me if I would be there.

"Hey, Brad, it's Paul," he said jauntily, oblivious to my crisis. "How's it going over there—are you going to the orientation tomorrow?"

"Hi, Paul, yeah, I'll probably see you there."

"Fine, sounds good," he said slowing down, as though he wanted to ask me something else. I then remembered he knew my wife was pregnant.

"Hey, do you all have a brand new baby over there yet?" he asked with a chuckle, no doubt expecting me to relate to him some charming story about the new baby.

"Well, Paul," I started again, getting ready to deliver the news to him, "I've got some bad news for you."

He was silent on the other end, then said uneasily, "What's that?"

"Well, our baby was stillborn. We lost him."

"Ohh!" Paul groaned, as though he had been punched in the stomach. "Oh, I'm so, so sorry. What happened?"

"I don't really know. We went to the doctor's office when my wife was over thirty-eight weeks pregnant, and there was no heartbeat."

Paul could tell I was fighting to hold back tears, and he said, "Well, I am so sorry, Brad."

He paused, my faint cries audible to him. I could tell he was befuddled as he uncomfortably cleared his throat.

"Well," he said, subdued, "I, uh, I hope it works out."

He said good-bye to me, then hung up the phone. I realized it was going to be very hard for me to talk to people the next day at orientation.

When I arrived at the classroom for the orientation, standing outside the door was the director of the writing program. We had never met. Evidently Patty had told her of my plight, because as she saw me walking into the classroom, she touched my shoulder and said, with a look of great sorrow on her face, "You must be Brad Stetson. I'm sorry about your loss."

Even the slightest remark like that would dislodge the tears I was constantly fighting to hold back. I thanked her for her sympathy, then sat down in the back of the room, crying softly.

Later that day, I had to stop by the offices of the department in which I was a graduate student. In the hallway I ran into a woman I knew. Her name was Rachel, and she was tall and good looking. She was also a graduate student and had been in a few classes of mine. I had noticed she wore a huge diamond on her left ring finger. She was fond of telling people her fiancé was a lawyer. She was a social worker at a large hospital. As I mechanically exchanged pleasantries with her, she said, casually popping the gum in her mouth, "Hey, wasn't your wife supposed to have a baby this summer?"

I felt weary from the stress of the day, having to go about my business while feeling such immense pain. But I responded to her directly, with the sentence that had become my standard line: "Yes, but unfortunately our baby was stillborn."

Rachel's reaction to this news was unlike any of the other people that day whom I had told. A gleaming smile flashed across her tanned face, and she said with obvious glee, "Oh, you're kidding, that's what I do—I work with people who've had that kind of stuff happen!"

She continued beaming at me, my overwhelming grief imperceptible to her. I nodded expressionlessly and turned away.

A few of my professors were in their offices, and although I liked and respected them, I rarely went to their offices to talk. I did not have a personal friendship with any of them. But now I felt drawn to their offices to visit each of them.

The first one I saw was an old gentleman, a favorite teacher of many of the students. His name was Dennis. He had white hair and smoked a pipe. He was smoking in his office when I knocked on his open door. He saw I didn't look well and told me to come in and sit down. I did, and without saying anything, started crying like a little boy.

"What is it, Brad, what's wrong?" Dennis said in a deep, soft, grandfatherly voice.

"Dennis, my wife was supposed to have a baby this summer, but he was stillborn. He died right before we were supposed to have him," I said through sobs, struggling to stop my tears.

"I'm sorry, Brad," Dennis said slowly, shaking his head. "It must be tough for you and your wife. You know, the same thing happened to my parents."

I looked up with interest.

"They had a baby before me, who died at birth. They never knew why it happened, what caused it."

"Oh, man," I said, wiping my face. "Did they ever take you to the grave when you were young?"

"No, they didn't," Dennis said. "Not until I was much older."

As I sat there, I started to feel foolish for walking into his office and spilling my guts to him. I got up to leave, and he said, "Why don't you go next door to Marvin's office? Maybe he knows a doctor or someone you could question about this kind of thing."

Marvin was a professor who was a medical ethicist. He knew a lot of doctors in the university's medical school, and the idea of talking with one of them, to try to get some answers for medical causes of "true knots," was appealing to me. I knocked on Marvin's door. He was an unkempt man, kind but rather brusque.

As soon as I knocked, he barked, "Come in."

I opened the door, and he swiveled in his chair, looking at me suspiciously.

"Hi, Marvin, could I talk to you for a second?"

I think he noticed I had been crying, because he immediately softened.

"Sure, sit. What is it?"

"Well," I began, knowing I was about to cry again, "my wife and I had a stillbirth a couple weeks ago. Our baby was stillborn, and, I . . ." I stopped, unable to finish my question.

He leaned forward, took off his glasses, and said, "Oh, I'm sorry about that. I'm very sorry."

I sniffed loudly and continued, "Dennis said you might know of a doctor in the medical school who might be able to talk to me about medical reasons for stillbirths?"

"Oh, yes," he said quickly, turning back to his desk and opening an address book. "Why don't you call Dr. Thomas Dale-Antoine. He teaches obstetrics, and he should be of some help to you." He told me the phone number. I wrote it down, then got up to leave.

"Sorry," I said, "to come in and interrupt you."

"Listen," Marvin said to me sternly as I stood in his doorway, "it's okay. You've suffered a terrible loss." I nodded at him, then left his office.

Those words "You've suffered a terrible loss" rang in my head. I repeated them to myself over and over. While it was something I already knew, the way he said it to me—the simplicity and accuracy of the statement—made a strong impact on me. It was then, as I left his office, that I began the process of accepting what had happened. "You've suffered a terrible loss" exactly described the reality in which Nina and I were living.

As I was on my way out of the department, I ran into one more professor. His name was Alan, and I knew he had once, long ago, been a chaplain in the Air Force. He was tall and thin and always looked ill. He had intense blue eyes, and he always looked directly at you when he spoke to you.

"Brad, I'm sorry about your baby," he said as he approached me. "Dennis told me what happened. I hope it works out for you. These next few months for you and your wife will be stressful, you know that."

I nodded, sensing he was trying to tell me something. His stare bored into me as he said, "I've known a lot of couples who have suffered similar tragedies. It really puts a strain on a marriage. You have to watch out for that."

He continued to stare at me, as if to make sure I understood.

"Yes, I know what you mean," I said quietly. Then I walked away.

I was done with everything I needed to do at school that day, but there was one more person I wanted to see before I left. His name was Winston Jackson, and he was a professor in the philosophy department at the university. He was a large, gentle man, with a soft Southern drawl and welcoming demeanor that had made him a favorite of many students. I also knew him to be a deeply spiritual Christian, and I was hoping to get a chance to speak with him about my grief and turmoil.

On my way over to his office, which was a good one-quarter mile from where I had been, I felt quite awful. I felt forgotten and neglected by God, as though he had been careless, asleep on the job, and this horrid thing had come upon Nina and me. As I walked, looking vacantly at the vibrant young college students passing in front of me, I remembered something that had happened to me on my first day of kindergarten.

I was four years old, and I was going to have to take the bus to my first day of school and then take it home afterward. This worried my mother immensely, so she took a number of precautions to make sure I would make it home on the bus safely.

A few days before kindergarten started, she drove over to my school. She showed it to me, and then, slowly, she drove home to our house, methodically pointing out to me various landmarks along the way, things I would recognize if I were lost, so I would be able to find my way home. I can still remember the slow droning of her voice as she said over and over, "You see that big pine tree, that's on the way home. You see that yellow house, that's on the way home to our house. You see those big oleander bushes, Brad, that's the street where you get off the bus. That street goes all the way to the street where we live." The street with the oleanders on the corner, which to my four-year-old mind looked like a vast forest of green, was called "Bigelow Park."

To make sure there was no mistaking which bus stop was mine, my mother constructed a large paper sign and hung it around my neck. She wrote in big black letters, "Bigelow Park." She put it on me before we left the house that first day of school, and she instructed me that under no circumstances was I to take the sign off. I was mortified. I spent the whole first day of kindergarten flinging the sign over my back, hoping my classmates were none the wiser.

After the first day of kindergarten successfully concluded, we were all issued lollipops—mine was orange—and herded onto our bus. Looking back, I don't know why I did it, but the first time the bus stopped—a considerable distance from the critical Bigelow Park—I happily bounded out. I have no idea why the bus driver let me go. The sign my mother had saddled me with could not be missed. Perhaps the driver was harried by all those squealing little children in her bus. After all, it was her first day of school too.

I can still vividly remember standing alone, on the sidewalk, watching the gigantic yellow bus rumble away belching black smoke. The last thing I saw was my neighbor and classmate Alfred Cohen—who was my seatmate on the bus and who was also supposed to get off at the magical Bigelow Park—pressing his little round face up against the window, his big brown eyes open wide as he shook his head and silently mouthed over and over, "No! No!"

Immediately I realized I had made a mistake and began to panic. Where was I? I knew the situation was serious. So I started walking down the sidewalk, looking at each house and bush, to see if I recognized it. Even today, three decades later, I can remember the powerful feelings of utter lostness, despair, panic, and hopelessness I felt as I aimlessly wandered alone down that street.

After a while I came across a woman pushing a baby stroller. "Wheya is Bigewoe Pock?" I asked earnestly.

The woman simply shook her head, said not a word, and walked on. I kept walking, and I became more and more frightened and bewildered. At last, up ahead I saw the magnificent oleanders of Bigelow Park. I turned down that street, knowing I was headed in the right direction. But this was a long street, and as I realized I wasn't finding my own street, I became frightened again. I sat down on the curb and sucked on my lollipop, crying. I was confused and scared. I hoped my mother would come by in her car and pick me up. After a while, I continued on and saw a house I recognized, which was on the corner of the street on which I lived. I turned onto my street, and my mother, who was standing outside of a neighbor's house, hysterically appealing to her for help in the search she was about to mount, saw me. She ran to me and swept me up in her arms.

As I made my way to Professor Jackson's office that day, I realized I felt much the same as I did long ago, trying to find my way home after my first day of kindergarten. Abandoned. No hope. Bewildered. Unsure of where my life was going.

As I walked into the philosophy department office, Professor Jackson was standing right in front of the secretary's desk, talking about a recipe or something. I heard him say, "I like them warm!" and then they both laughed uproariously.

"Professor Jackson?" I said tentatively as I stood just inside the doorway.

He turned and saw me, and instantly the broad smile vanished from his face and a look of sober inquisitiveness replaced it.

"Yes, Brad, what is it?" he said, as the secretary headed into an adjoining room.

"Can I talk to you, please?"

"Yes, of course," he said. "Let's go out here to the courtyard."

This courtyard was a beautiful stone and brick garden area surrounded on three sides by the philosophy building, a magnificent old structure—perhaps a century old—which had the names of great philosophers inscribed in its side all the way around the building, up high where the walls join the eaves: Thales, Pythagoras, Zeno, Plato, Aristotle, Cicero, Augustine, Aquinas, Scotus, Descartes, Hobbes, Spinoza, and on and on. Menacing-looking gargoyles stared down from their perches near the roof, and Jesus' words "The Truth Shall Make You Free" were carved into the side of one wall overlooking the courtyard. It was late morning, not too hot, and a large honeysuckle bush in the middle of the courtyard provided a beautiful scent. Professor Jackson and I strolled over to a cement bench in the shade of the building and sat down.

He was tall and hefty but had a perceptible air of gentleness and self-control about him. He was also brilliant. Although he was a world-class philosopher and could easily have talked over the heads of students, graduate students, and most of his colleagues, he never did. Frequently he offered homespun wisdom and advice, always with the utmost tact and sincerity.

"What is it, Brad? I can see you're upset," Jackson said sympathetically, looking at me, his arms crossed.

Again I explained my plight as I fought back tears, trying to control myself.

"Oh, dear, oh Brad, I'm sorry about that," Jackson slowly said, taking his glasses off and rubbing his eyes, his head bent down.

"I'm wondering why this happened," I said, slowly recovering my composure.

"Well, that's the big question, isn't it?" He stopped to draw a big breath. "You'll never really know, but it may be that this was for the best."

I looked at him, surprised.

He continued, "You don't know what might have happened to your son. Maybe he would have become a drug addict and killed himself, or maybe he would have suffered terribly with some horrible disease. You know, years ago this same thing happened to a couple I knew. Their full-term baby was stillborn."

"What did they tell you they learned through that experience?"

"How precious life is. That's it, just how absolutely precious life is and how every moment should be cherished and savored."

We sat in silence.

"Brad," he finally said to me, "I think you and your wife should try to take things easy for a while. Try to enjoy life. Take walks on the beach, go about things slowly, don't make any big, important decisions about your life right now, just try to see things settle down. You've been through a lot, and the next few months or even years won't be easy for you."

"I know," I said, rubbing my eyes. "My wife's sister is pregnant now too. She's having her baby any day now, just a couple weeks after we were supposed to have our baby. I'm afraid . . ." I paused, wondering what words to use. "I'm afraid her baby will always remind us about ours, that he'll always be a painful symbol to us of all we lost."

Jackson looked at me and said in a strong voice, "You don't have to understand him that way; you don't have to look at your sister-in-law's baby that way, not at all."

Again there was a moment of silence.

"You know, Brad," he said, still looking at me, "I want to caution you about feeling angry at God for this. It's natural and understandable that you might feel that way, but—"

"I do feel that way," I interrupted, speaking with a fervor that surprised me.

"But you don't know his purposes, his—"

"What purpose could there possibly be in this?" I nearly yelled.

He paused as a slightly pained look came across his face. "Just because you can't see one doesn't mean that there isn't one. Do you think God is good?"

I was surprised by the question, but he was clearly waiting for an answer from me, so I said, subdued, "Yes."

"Do you think God is all powerful?"

I waited, then answered, "Yes."

"Does not God, by definition, know everything?"

"I guess he must."

"Is God moral or immoral?" he asked again, speaking a little more rapidly.

"Well, moral."

"Then I take it you would agree God is fair and just?" he said, looking deeply into my eyes.

I looked away, and said, almost reluctantly, "I know that God is fair and just.

"Well, Brad," he said without waiting, "you're going to have to realize that God, being wholly good, fair, and just, is not a worthy target for your anger. You suffered a tragedy. That does happen in this world. You're not the first person to suffer like this; you won't be the last. Does life come with a guarantee on it that we will never experience personal catastrophes and tragic losses? If it does, I never got my copy."

"Brad," he continued, "never forget that God is fair. I really want to emphasize that. He is fair and just and does not allow unfairness or injustice to ultimately prevail in the lives of people or in the universe itself. While at the moment it may seem to you that there is no moral order or reason in the world, that is emphatically not the case. No matter what happens to you in your life, always remember the justice of God. It is one idea which will save you a lot of anguish, and, more than any other thought, will preserve your psychological health."

I nodded slowly. "But why—you know, I just can't get that question out of my head—why did this happen?"

"Well, beyond any medical information you may have received about the biological causes for this, you'll probably never really know. Not in this life anyway."

I sat concentrating on what he was telling me, so that I would be able to remember it.

Then, looking straight ahead, Jackson said to me, "Have you ever read the story of the blind man healed by Jesus, in chapter nine of the gospel of John?"

"Uh, yeah, but I'm not sure I remember the details."

"Well, the man had been blind from birth, and Jesus healed him. Do you think after the man was healed by Jesus he regretted having been blind?"

"Well," I said, puzzled, "I don't know. Maybe."

Jackson smiled and said, "Well, you should think about that, because I don't think so. Right before Jesus healed the blind man, he said that the man's blindness happened so that the work of God might be displayed in the blind man's life. Have you stopped to consider that perhaps this happened to you so that the work of God might be displayed in your life in a manner it otherwise might not ever have been?"

I sat in silence, thinking about his words. "Professor Jackson," I said after a few seconds, "where is my son now? I mean, I know he's dead, but—"

Jackson interrupted me, saying with certainty, "He's not dead."

I looked at him, and he looked at me. I didn't know exactly what he meant.

"Well—" I started, but was interrupted again by the professor.

"He's not dead. You need to do some work on this idea. Do you not have a soul, or is your body all you are?"

"I think I am more than just my body. I'm that, plus—"

"Well, so is your son," Jackson interjected. "The body he lived in died. He himself did not. He lives on. Physical death is not the end of life. Quite the contrary, it is the beginning of life indeed. I like what the evangelist Dwight Moody said near the end of his days on earth: 'One day soon you will hear that I am dead. Do not believe it. I will then be alive as never before.'"

I felt an odd sense of happiness and encouragement surge into me, something I had not felt since that horrible moment in Dr. Lloyd's office.

"He's with God, isn't he?" I said with a slight smile.

"Indeed he is," Jackson said, nodding his head.

"But how do you know exactly?"

Jackson chuckled heartily and stood up, gently slapping my leg as he did. "Brad, some things are axiomatic. They're so basic you just naturally know they're true."

I stood up with him, realizing our conversation had come to an end.

"Well, thank you, Professor," I said as we walked back toward the philosophy department.

He turned to me. "Please take things easy, Brad. Remember to do that. It's going to take time before you feel any better. Okay? Talk honestly with God and other people, especially your wife. That's going to help."

"Thanks, Professor Jackson," I said, shaking his hand.

As he went inside, I walked away, back through the courtyard. I was very glad I had the chance to talk with him. While I didn't feel significantly better than I had before I spoke with him, I did feel relief. I sensed it had been an important conversation, and I made a point in my mind to remember what he said to me.

CHAPTER II

Grieving Badly

*A*s the fateful month of August ended and September began, Nina and I both tried to resume our lives. We knew we had no choice but to do so. We were slogging through a psychological and emotional swamp of sorrow, though, and it was a struggle for us. We were on a sort of existential autopilot, living from habit rather than any vital awareness of our lives.

An important help to both of us was the many sympathy cards and expressions of condolence we received. I had never before realized or understood the importance of sympathy cards. I had always thought them an empty but polite gesture. But now, even the stiffest, most trite Hallmark cards, the ones that just said in elaborate cursive, "Thinking of You," were surprisingly helpful to us. It said to us that people cared, that in a distant, imperfect way, they understood the magnitude of what had happened to us, and they felt for us. It truly helped to know that. Occasionally Nina and I would pull them all out of the drawer we kept them in and read them over.

I remember one day I received a letter in the mail from the Philippines. I noticed it had first been sent to Pastor Ed at church, and he had forwarded it to me. I opened it up. It was a brief note of sympathy from Eric and Debbie Sandalero, missionaries our church supported who lived in someplace called Davao City, Philippines. Ed had told them what happened to us, and even though they didn't know us, Debbie had taken the time to write a note. It said, "Brad and Nina, Ed told us of the loss of your baby boy. We are very sorry for you. You'll be in our prayers, and the church here is praying for you as well."

I wept as I stood in my kitchen reading that simple note. *BJ's life touched somebody all the way over in the Philippines,* I thought. That fact was a great comfort to me. It said to me his life meant something; he was not just an unknown, anonymous baby that had never made it out of the womb, forgotten by all but his parents. No, even on the other side of the world, the impact of his life and loss were felt.

As the fall leaves changed color and papered the ground—a fitting symbol of our faded hopes and downcast hearts—I realized that Nina and I would need to allow ourselves to grieve truly. We should not suppress our emotions behind a sunny facade and pretend we really felt fine when we did not. We would have to yield to the natural pain of great loss, and permit ourselves to authentically experience this deepest of human hurts. We could not hurry the process and get it done on our own timetable, but rather would simply have to live, trusting that the disorienting turbulence of mourning would subside in due course, and we would settle into a new and different way of living and thinking.

But such equanimity is easier to understand than apply, and in truth, Nina and I endured this immensely difficult period of our lives in ways that were not always healthy.

Nina continued working with her kindergarten class, staying late after school to work in her room, preparing teaching materials at home during the night, and generally diverting her outward attention from our loss. But inwardly, of course, she was completely heartbroken. She would come home from school sometimes, telling me of how much it hurt to see mothers at her school carrying young babies. Sometimes one of them, who knew she had been pregnant, would see her, notice she wasn't pregnant anymore, and ask how her baby was. Nina would politely—and stoically—tell them what had happened. But she would cry intensely as she would relate these events to me. Frequently in the evenings she would just start crying without saying anything. I would hold her and cry with her, but it was mild comfort to her. She had lost her firstborn, and she would not be exactly the same person anymore.

Those first few months I especially noticed a loss in her short-term memory. She would forget where she had placed her keys just a minute earlier; she would have to look up phone numbers she used to know by heart; she would forget appointments.

Once I called to have a termite inspector come to our house. I couldn't be there on the afternoon he was to come by, which was in about a week's time, so I reminded Nina for the whole week not to forget the appointment with the termite man. Sure enough, the evening of the day he was to come by, I came home and asked Nina how it went. She looked at me blankly and said, embarrassed, "I completely forgot about it."

In retrospect, it certainly would have been helpful to us if we had both been in counseling. But, unfortunately, we weren't at that time. It simply hadn't occurred to us, no one around us had suggested it, and we were both reluctant to talk in detail about losing BJ and how we felt, at least not to anyone but ourselves. But to have been in a setting where we could, separately or together, honestly talk through our deepest feelings and fears would have been extremely soothing for us.

While Nina remained generally stoic and outwardly unchanged by the stress of grief, I did not. The sight of a baby on television or a mother with a child was enough to make me cry. I began to gain weight, and each day I seemed to feel worse than I had the day before.

For four months after losing BJ, I visited the cemetery each day. Every day I cleaned the tablet, replaced the flowers, sat near it, and generally doted on it.

One day around Thanksgiving, as I was scrubbing away on the tablet trying to remove a boot print someone had left on it, I remembered what Naomi Estrada had once told me.

She was an acquaintance of a friend of mine from college. Back then, when I would go over to my friend's apartment to see him, she would occasionally be there. She was an elderly lady, probably about sixty-five. She had been a mortician in East Los Angeles, at her family's funeral home. She would periodically relate stories—usually very depressing—of her experiences at work. But she seemed to enjoy telling them, so we would sit and listen to her.

Once she told us of the reconstruction job she had done on the face of a baby who had been born with a terrible facial deformation and had died soon after birth. The baby's face was essentially nonexistent, and Naomi, even though the grieving family had not asked her to, refashioned the infant's face out of plaster of paris and other materials, creating quite a realistic and lifelike rendering of what the baby would have looked like had he been born normally formed. At the viewing of the body before the funeral—which was to be held at her mortuary—the devastated parents of the baby saw what Naomi had done and were overwhelmed with both gratitude to her for her work, and sorrow at seeing this glimpse of what their precious child might have looked like. Naomi described the emotional reactions of the parents, how they lay on the floor of the chapel, crying hysterically, and finally had to be lifted up by the pallbearers and placed in a pew.

After Naomi had finished this story, I insensitively and ignorantly said to her, "What was the big deal? So the parents saw a fake face?"

Naomi looked at me with cold anger, then said in a low, controlled voice, "Wait until it happens to you. Wait until you lose somebody, and then you'll know what it's like."

As I sat next to BJ's tablet, I thought of her words, "Wait until it happens to you." Well, it had happened to me all right, ultimate tragedy had visited me and my house, and I remembered how grateful that baby's family was to Naomi for what she had done. I understood why.

As I was sitting there on the damp grass recalling that conversation with Naomi, I heard a man behind me say, "Muevelo, muevelo."

I stood up, startled, and spun around to see a Hispanic man of about sixty. He reeked of alcohol and was obviously drunk. He kept mumbling to himself as he walked, stopping about thirty feet away from me in front of another tablet in the urn garden. He turned around toward me, pointing down at the tablet, and said in broken and slurred English, "My son. This is my son."

The tablet he was pointing to was that of Ernesto Lopez Jr., who died at age thirty-five. I noticed that tablet the day of BJ's memorial service. I realized I was talking to the senior Ernesto Lopez. I said, "I'm sorry," but he continued mumbling, walking in circles around his son's grave, alternately crying and yelling.

I knew it would be hard to communicate to him, but I walked over to him and said in a loud, slow voice, "I'm sorry about your son. It must be very hard for you."

He stopped walking in circles and stared at me. He took a step toward me. I noticed in his hand a paper bag wrapped around a bottle, and I thought he might strike me with it. I took a step back, and he said to me, much clearer, "He died. My son died in Pittsburgh."

My fear faded and I said sincerely, my head tilted slightly to one side, "I'm so sorry. I'm sorry."

Then, still looking at me with his somewhat wild eyes, he said clearly again, "He froze. My son froze to death."

He then turned around back to the grave and fell to his knees, sobbing uncontrollably. I knew our conversation was over, and I certainly didn't want to press him for an explanation. I concluded his son had been homeless and froze to death one winter on the streets of Pittsburgh.

Before I started to leave, I took a few steps closer to Ernesto Lopez Jr.'s tablet, and I noticed the date of death was sometime in November of 1989. *That was two years ago,* I thought, *and the father is still in this state of emotional disarray.* As I walked to my car, I feared that would be my fate too.

The next day when I arrived at the cemetery, I stood beside BJ's grave again for a while, then decided to go for a walk around the grounds. I had always wondered about some large monuments off to one side, so I walked toward them.

They were family plots. I came to one, a large granite marker, about five feet high and three feet wide. Across the top, in capital letters, was written MITCHELL. Across the bottom of the marker was a list of five names. They were first names and middle names, each followed by a birth date and a death date. As I stood staring at this old granite slab, I noticed the dates were just a few years apart: 1881–1883; 1884–1885; 1886–1889; 1889–1889; 1901–1911. My heart sank and my knees buckled, as I realized these had been the Mitchells' children. They had lost all five, most of them during the first couple years of their lives. At the very bottom of the slab, beneath this roster of sadness, were the names of Mr. and Mrs. Mitchell and the simple statement, "At Rest." *What profound, incomprehensible suffering they endured,* I thought. *How did they manage?*

I continued walking around the cemetery. It was so vast, with so many graves, I found it difficult to focus on any single one. It was a bright southern California day in late November. Out of the corner of my eye, I spotted a ray of sun glinting on a small black tablet. I walked over to it. It was half overgrown with weeds, and part of it was covered with silt. I kneeled down, pulled the weeds back, and blew hard, my breath clearing away the light silt. The black marker read:

> *Elizabeth Ann Brown*
> August 10, 1988—August 12,1988
> Our Little Angel

I immediately started crying. She had only lived two days. How awful. But even more than that, what disturbed me was that her grave seemed neglected. I visualized BJ's grave looking like that, as though I had forgotten about him and ignored his life. I said aloud, crying quite hard, "I will not forget about BJ, I will not forget about BJ."

I got up after a few minutes and walked on. But as I did, I wondered if perhaps I was wrong about the Browns having neglected their child's grave. Maybe they had simply moved on with their lives. Maybe they'd survived and returned to a normal—albeit different—pattern of living and saw no productive purpose served by hanging around the cemetery. Perhaps they had processed their loss and now looked to the future, not the past. Such sentiments were not incompatible with the full and respectful remembrance of their daughter, I realized. "Life is for the living, isn't it," I said out loud to myself.

Just as I was about to turn around, I noticed off to one side a large old headstone. I went over and stood in front of it. It was the grave of an eighteen-year-old boy, who had died one hundred years ago, in 1891. I stood there and looked at it and thought of his parents. I then noticed, engraved into the top of the headstone, in small letters that had almost been weathered away, a poem. I read it out loud, straining to make out the faint words:

> *God knows why, with chilling touch,*
> *Death gathers those we love so much.*
> *And what now seems so strange and dim,*
> *Will all be clear, when we know Him.*

After I finished, I paused and read it again. "So strange and dim." Those words rang so totally true to me. It was all so strange. Perverse, even. That BJ would live inside of his mother for nine months, only to die on the eve of his birth, because of his own umbilical cord, his source of sustenance. My eyes settled on the word *dim*. I did not understand why we had lost BJ. My vision of my future, my wife's, life itself seemed dim and cloudy to me. My life was indeed strange and dim.

The opening words of that poem, "God knows why," were a comfort to me though, as if promising everything would work out in the end. Not that the pain would be washed away, but that meaning and understanding would be restored to the world and to my life. The sovereign control of God over what seem the aimless vicissitudes of this life would some day—perhaps in the fullest sense only post-mortem—be apparent, and reasons and explanations for tragedies would be presented and understood. God knows why things happen, I thought to myself, and in his mercy he will not forever allow his children to be tormented by ambiguity and confusion. I gazed at the poem for another fifteen minutes or so, trying to memorize it. As I walked away, I repeated it to myself again.

As I drove home, I realized I was emotionally exhausted and deeply depressed. Going to the cemetery day after day, for more than ninety days, had taken a terrible toll on me. I was literally draining myself away. A spiritual weakness permeated my body.

Adding to my trouble, I had become an insomniac, sleeping only about four or five hours a night. I spent long hours staring at the television, mindlessly flipping through our cable channels. My mind was filled with the banal scripts of infomercials. I was especially annoyed by the late-night visage of an ebullient, millionaire real-estate investor named Bill Lu, who in chopped English nightly crowed from atop his deluxe yacht, surrounded by beautiful women in bikinis, "Come to my seminar! Come to my seminar!" He advertised happiness and money to anyone who would attend this celebration of avarice. His apparently carefree life of success, wealth, and recreation mocked my own experience of existential paralysis, dank depression, and abysmal sorrow. I developed a strange anger at this man, routinely muttering "Shut up" at the television whenever I saw him.

I was also, I knew, a lazy and ineffective writing teacher, never preparing any lessons for my students. I could tell they hated coming to class. And I had gained about twenty-five pounds in the three months or so since BJ's stillbirth.

The stress of grieving in this way had also begun to have an effect on my relationship with Nina. As December began, we started fighting with each other more and more. Usually the subjects of our arguments were themselves insignificant. They were only surrogates for the deeper frustration and pain each of us felt.

A typical episode occurred one afternoon before Nina returned home from school. I was hungry—and bored—so I had decided to eat dinner early. I went out and bought myself a large pizza and was sitting in front of the television wolfing it down when she arrived home about 4:30.

"What are you doing?" she asked in an irritated voice.

"What does it look like I'm doing?" I turned toward her and growled, with a mouth full of pizza.

"I was going to cook tonight!" she exclaimed. "Didn't you see that chicken sitting on the counter? I was going to cook that!"

She then threw her school bag down on the kitchen counter and slammed a few drawers in the kitchen. Drawer slamming was a sure way to anger me. So I leaped up and stormed into the kitchen.

"What's the big deal, Nina?" I yelled. "I didn't see the chicken, all right?"

"It's sitting right in front of you. Are you blind or something?"

"So put the chicken away, you can use it again later."

"Great," she said, still furious, "and what am *I* going to eat now?"

She saw that I had already devoured the entire pizza.

"All right," I said, blushing a little bit, "I'll go get you something. What do you want?"

"I don't want anything, I'll take care of myself," she snapped, slamming a few more drawers.

"Will you stop slamming the drawers, Nina? What's the point of that?"

"You are so selfish, Brad!" she shrieked. "All you ever do is think about yourself!"

"Nina, that's not true, you don't need to say that."

"You know it's true," she said, now looking directly at me, her face red with rage. "You've always been that way."

"Why do you have to be so mean? It's not my fault if you had a bad day," I said, starting to sense that I was getting angrier.

"Oh no, nothing is ever your fault," she said sarcastically, emphatically waving her hands. "You always do the right thing, everyone knows that."

I snapped.

"Listen to me," I said in a quiet voice, looking down at her and sticking my index finger in her face, the way I would do when I was enraged. "You're trying to blame me for how you feel. You're trying to blame me for the situation you're in."

My furious gaze burned into her. We were quiet for moment, in a stare down.

"What do you mean, the 'situation' I'm in?" she said, stomping over to the sink. She began to wash dishes, scrubbing with great energy. "What 'situation' do you think I'm in, huh?"

she yelled over her shoulder. "You don't know what you're talking about, you don't know anything about how I feel."

"Listen, Nina," I said firmly, feeling like I was about to cry as I walked over to her and stood next to her. "It's not my fault you're lonely and angry, okay? *I* didn't do anything," I said, jabbing my index finger into her arm.

She stopped washing, put her wet hands on her hips, and turned to me.

"What do you mean, *I* didn't do anything. What's that supposed to mean? Huh? What's that supposed to mean?"

She turned away and began crying, leaning over the sink. After a few minutes, she picked up her keys and purse, stormed out of the house, and sped away in her car.

We both knew what it meant when I said things like "*I* didn't do anything." These arguments frequently came to such a climax, where I would subtly blame Nina for BJ's death, and in some way imply that she'd been irresponsible. Obviously a horrible, terrible thing to do. On rare occasions, she would return the favor and say things like, "Well, if you weren't always telling me to be careful or telling me I couldn't do something, maybe I would have been more relaxed!"

Nina and I both knew that neither one of us was responsible for BJ's stillbirth. Furthermore, we both knew that we knew. But the strain of grief, the pain of loss, and the prolonged nature of our emotional agony set the stage for such hurtful exchanges.

While Nina and I had only talked about it occasionally, the truth was we ached for another child. This fact underlay much of our hostility. We desperately wanted to try to have another child as soon as we could, but Dr. Lloyd had told us we should wait three months before trying to conceive in order to minimize any risk of miscarriage. Of course, being unable to even try to get pregnant only added to our frustration.

While we knew that we could not have a baby that would replace BJ, or one, God forbid, that would make us forget about BJ, we still had a simple, pure, persistent desire to try to have another child. We knew it was dangerous to try to medicate our pain by having another child, and we had each agreed that we would not fall into that trap. If we had another baby, we would not name him BJ, nor would we use another child to somehow seek to circumvent the natural, painful development of our emotions. That would not be healthy for us or for a new baby. Quite to the contrary, we consciously thought of our hoped-for baby as someone who would affirm to us all BJ meant. She would be a monument to our love for BJ and each other, a recognition of our loss and our God-given will to survive, and, most of all, a precious gift in her own right. She would be an individual, ordained by God and called to the fullness of her own life in him. But we seemed so far away from such a glorious gift. I sometimes feared we would never have another child. The simple truth was that our future was unclear, and we could not control it.

When Nina came back into the house about forty-five minutes later, I was standing in the upstairs bathroom, staring blankly at myself in the mirror. I knew I had been wrong to say such a terrible thing, and as I heard her come in, I knew I would have to apologize to her. I went downstairs. She was in the kitchen washing dishes again. I walked up to her and kissed her shoulder.

She shrugged her shoulder and said, still upset, "Get away from me." I stepped back.

"Honey," I said, now calm, "I'm sorry. I'm sorry for what I said to you." I waited to see her reaction. She continued scrubbing. "I know you did everything right with BJ. I know you were a perfect mommy to him."

She stopped scrubbing, her head drooped, her hands fell to her sides, and leaning up against the counter, she began sobbing. She turned around and we embraced, both of us crying hard.

"I miss BJ, I miss him!" Nina sobbed, her body shaking. "I wish we had him."

"I know, honey, I wish we did too."

I wiped her tears on my T-shirt, and she said, "I went to BJ's grave when I left. You've been taking good care of it, honey. The flowers are nice."

I said, "Let's go sit down for a while."

Just as we were leaving the kitchen, the phone rang. Nina picked it up.

"Hello."

I was looking at her face, and suddenly a look of pain and anguish came over her face as she listened to the caller.

"No, I can't use any diaper coupons," she said, obviously upset.

"Hang up the phone!" I urged.

Nina was still holding the receiver up to her ear as she started crying, saying, "Well, yes, I did have a baby, but I don't have one now. I don't need any diaper coupons."

She hung up the phone, sobbing again. I walked over to her and hugged her, then dragged her over to the couch.

This had happened many times before. Salesmen, who must have obtained our number off a roster of Lamaze students or a baby store mailing list or something, would call, wanting us to buy diapers, formula, baby clothes and toys, all kinds of things. We would also get ads in the mail. These encounters were, of course, extremely painful. I had for weeks been screening the mail before Nina got home from work, searching for ads with baby pictures on them, ads for baby magazines or parent magazines, coupons for baby formula, and so on, throwing them in the trash so she wouldn't see them. But occasionally phone calls like that would reach her, and it was always very upsetting.

Nina and I spent that night on the couch together, relaxing. Often, as she and I would sit there together, I would almost compulsively think of BJ's ashes, buried in that cold, wet grave, while we sat in our warm living room, without him. If only he were with us, as he should have been.

When it came time for Nina to go to bed that night, I went upstairs with her. I sat on the bed watching television as she brushed her teeth. Her nightgown was on the bed. I picked it up and held it as she got herself ready for the night. She walked over to me and asked for her nightgown. "Not until you take your clothes off," I said.

Nina and I had rarely been intimate in the preceding few months, but tonight it seemed right to me.

She took a step back from me and looked at me with her dark eyes, a flicker of playfulness in them. I watched her as she got undressed. For the first time since she had BJ, I looked closely at her naked body. She was two feet away from me, and in the well-lit room I saw she was different.

Her body had changed. She now had the body of a woman who had had a child—the body of a mother. Her breasts, hips, stomach, buns, and thighs all testified to her journey from conception to childbirth. I realized as I looked at her that she had invested all of herself in BJ—her spirit, mind, *and* body. She had given of herself to him in the most complete way, and the impact he had on her life extended to her physical body, leaving unique marks and shapes that bore witness to her powerful love for him, and to her profound, total commitment to his life.

Nina stepped forward. Sitting on the edge of the bed, I embraced her, pressing my ear gently into her belly, as I once did to listen for BJ. Now, I heard only Nina's steady heartbeat, and the living sounds of her transformed body.

Chapter 12

Proper Understanding

*I*n the following month, December, grief began to truly choke me. It had me in its grip, and each day I felt its tendrils tighten. The days seemed to be getting longer to me, even though the December sunset was in the early evening hours. The dark, dreary clouds and intermittent rain funneled me deeper into depression.

I began to realize that I was feeling worse, not better. I was sinking in a quicksand of grief. Time did not seem to be my ally. I had expected that the worst part of my sorrow would be the days immediately after BJ's birth and funeral, and that then, as the weeks rolled by, I would gradually start to feel better. But in fact, my emotional and psychological state had steadily deteriorated.

Nina, though, seemed to be doing better. She frequently had long, tearful conversations with her mother and two sisters, and these hours-long talks helped her express her complex emotions. She was integrating her feelings into herself, honestly facing the painful truth of her situation. She also found great solace caring for her nieces and nephews— baby-sitting them or just visiting with them. This surprised me. The sight of children was hurtful to me, but Nina, perhaps because of her unquenchable drive for motherhood and fierce love for children, appreciated being around them, whether at work or at home.

As my semester at USC drew to a close, I had more time. On a day I knew I would be free, I made an appointment with Dr. Thomas Dale-Antoine, the professor of obstetrics who had been recommended by Marvin, the professor. I was still obsessed with finding an answer to why BJ's cord had grown so long and formed a "true knot." I was hoping Dr. Dale-Antoine would have an explanation.

That morning as I left my house, it was raining again. I stopped by the cemetery on my way to see Dr. Dale-Antoine. As I approached BJ's tablet, I saw that the rain had scrubbed it clean. It looked rather majestic, I thought, as I looked at the bright white letters etched into the dark red stone. Standing there, holding my umbrella, I thought of my parents.

They were grieving too, I knew. They had never communicated that to me, but I knew that they were devastated, and that they yearned for grandchildren. They didn't come down to visit us as much as they had when Nina was pregnant.

Perhaps it was just too painful for them. I could not shake the stubborn feeling that I had disappointed them. I remembered the look my mother's face assumed when I had disappointed her as a child—part heartbreak, part angry frown. It was an intense expression, and in my mind's eye I clearly saw it as I stood at the grave. It looked the same as it had when I was sixteen and failed my test for a driver's license.

My mother had taken me down to the local DMV office. She gave me a little pep talk as we stood by her car waiting for the DMV examiner to come and put me through the paces.

"Just remember to signal every time you turn, and relax, you can do it. Just do everything the best you can and you'll pass," she assured me, although I detected a tinge of doubt in her exhortation.

When the DMV man came over to our car, my mother's stick-shift Honda Accord, he said nothing to me except in a weary voice, "Let's go." He was a tall man, with old-fashioned black-rimmed glasses and gray hair. He wore one of those pocket protectors in his shirt pocket, and it was full of pens and sharpened pencils. *A by-the-book nerd,* I thought. This made me even more nervous than I already was.

The whole test actually went quite well—until the end. In front of the DMV office—which was at a busy four-way intersection—I attempted to turn left on the green light, against oncoming traffic. Inexplicably I pulled out in front of a UPS delivery truck, which skillfully swerved to its right, barely missing us. It would still have hit us and probably killed the poor DMV employee, had he not, with impressive quickness, pulled the emergency break with his left hand just as I started my ill-advised turn. As the big brown truck rumbled by, the irritated UPS driver scowled at me and called, "Watch out!"

The DMV man closed his eyes, exhaled loudly, and said, "That'll do it. Go back."

A minute later when I pulled into the DMV driveway, my mother was waiting for us. She had a hopeful look on her face. As I stopped, the DMV man, in one motion, jumped out of the car and handed my mom a pink paper, saying over his shoulder as he walked away briskly, "He needs more work."

My mom leaned in the car and said to me, with that unforgettable expression on her face, "What did you do?"

That exasperated question echoed in my mind as I stood there at BJ's grave in the rain.

"God," I said out loud, "I pray my parents would find some peace about BJ. I ask you to allow them to live to see their grandchildren, and I pray you would bless us with another child. I pray that you'll help Nina and me to conceive again. In Jesus' name, amen."

As I drove up to Dr. Dale-Antoine's office, I thought about what I would ask him. For some reason I imagined he would be very helpful, offer me literature, show me pictures, give me understanding.

Such was not the case. After I had waited for an hour and fifteen minutes, a woman showed me back to his office. It was a large room with papers strewn everywhere. I sat down in an empty spot on an old couch. Dr. Dale-Antoine, a fit, swarthy man of about forty-five, was on the phone talking about golf courses. It seemed he and the person on the other end of the line were making a golf appointment. After a few minutes he hung up. He turned around in his chair and said, "Yes, what can I do for you?" like he didn't know why I was there.

"Well, uh, Dr. Dale-Antoine," I stammered, "I, uh, I came to talk to you about my wife."

"Where's your wife?" he asked suspiciously.

"She's at work," I answered quickly.

"Why are you here?" he asked.

"We had a stillbirth recently," I blurted out, sensing he wanted me to get to the point. "I just, uh, I just was wondering if you had any answers as to why this happened, what causes this kind of thing. The umbilical cord was very long, well over 125 centimeters, and—"

"You know," he interrupted as he leaned back in his chair and placed his hands behind his head, "I would need to see her records before I could—"

His phone rang loudly. He reached over and picked it up, looking me over.

He had a blank expression on his face as he listened. I could hear only his part of the conversation.

"Oh yes, I know Dr. Francis, he's a good friend. . . . Okay, how far along are you? . . . Oh that's no problem, you're early. . . . Oh, not long at all. Since you're only nine weeks, the actual procedure is only twenty minutes or so. Afterwards we'll keep you around a bit for observation, but then you can go."

I looked away from him.

He continued. "Oh, you're in New York City, what show are you in? . . . And that's at the Wintergreen Theater now? Oh yes, that's right, my wife and I were there not long ago. She loves Broadway shows. . . . Well, listen, you have to do what's best for you. . . . Okay, just give my office a call. Bye-bye now."

I was appalled he was making abortion appointments while I was trying to speak with him about the stillbirth of our precious son. I suddenly felt that talking with him about BJ was an insult to BJ's memory, and I knew that, at any rate, Dr. Dale-Antoine's recognition of the unspeakable value of human fetal life was lacking. I understood he would not be a source of wisdom or insight.

He hung up the phone and turned back to me, saying hurriedly, "Sir, I don't think I can help you. You know, these things are just bad luck." He stood up and walked over to a stack of papers, paging through them. "It's like walking out into the street and getting hit by a truck. It just happens sometimes; there's nothing you can do about it. I think you and your wife should just try to get on with your lives. Forget about this."

He turned toward me, looked at me, and said with his eyebrows raised, "Okay?"

Realizing our conversation was over, I thanked him for his time and left. The disappointment I felt only added to my frustration. Dismay was added to this mix of emotions, when, a few days later, I received the bill for my ten-minute "consultation" with Dr. Dale-Antoine: $300.

When I arrived home after my fruitless meeting with Dr. Dale-Antoine, I plopped onto the couch exhausted and started to read the local newspaper. It was a small community paper that usually packed its pages with stories of school kids winning awards, Little League baseball scores, and high school football action. If anything of any civic significance happened, it would say so, but only in the barest detail.

To my surprise, as I was paging through the paper I saw the headline, "Local Woman Hit by Truck, Killed."

I read the story immediately, stunned to see that the victim was Cecilia Martin, a longtime friend of my mother. According to this news story, she had been hit by a speeding tow truck and killed instantly. She had been out walking her dog just after sunset, was crossing (inside the crosswalk) a busy street near her house, and, for some reason, didn't notice the tow truck coming. And obviously, the driver didn't notice her. The article didn't give much information about the accident but enough for me to visualize the event. Oh, the moment of abject horror and fear she must have felt when she looked up and realized this tow truck was going to hit her.

I felt nauseous and dazed. Death had struck once again. Chilled, I put my hands over my face and said slowly, "No, No."

I knew I was going to have to call my mother and tell her this disastrous news. Cecilia had been a close friend of hers. She would want to know about this, but it was going to be deeply upsetting to her.

Without reflecting on it any further, I went to the phone and punched in my parents' number.

"Hello," my mom said.

"Hi, Mom, it's Brad."

"Yes, honey, what is it?" she asked, already sounding apprehensive. She had learned to fear calls from me ever since I called to give her the news about BJ.

"Well, look, I have some bad news for you."

"What is it?" she said, already upset.

"Well, I'm reading the newspaper here, and apparently last night Cecilia Martin was hit by a truck and killed."

"And killed?" she shrieked.

"Yes," I said, as she began weeping and sobbing, just as she had done when I told her of her grandson's death.

I told her I would let her know if I found out when the memorial service was, but she was so upset I don't think she heard me. Quickly we said good-bye, and she hung up, still sobbing.

I felt terrible about telling her this news, but I couldn't have simply pretended not to know about it. That friendship was important to her. I thought about the impact this tragedy would have on Cecilia's family and on my mother, and I became angry. How could the driver have run over someone in the crosswalk?

Where before my reaction to death was mainly subdued and broken, now I was angry beyond description. I have never before felt such fury.

I pulled the telephone book out and looked up the number of the tow trunk company, which had been named in the article. I found it and dialed.

"Yeah," a gruff voice answered.

"I want to speak to the operations manager please," I said, my voice trembling with sheer anger.

"That would be me. What can I do for ya," the voice said. I pictured a grizzled, greasy man.

"I see one of your drivers killed a pedestrian last night. Don't you teach them not to do that?"

"Well, yeah, we do, as a matter of fact," he said defiantly. "Who is this?"

"Listen, that doesn't matter." I swore at him. "Why are your drivers so irresponsible? Why don't they know what they're doing?"

"All right, thanks for calling," the man said calmly, then hung up.

I slammed the receiver down, picked up my car keys, and went out to my car, slamming the door behind me. I was in a state of apoplectic rage.

I got in my car and peeled away. I don't know why I started driving around; that wasn't a very smart thing to do feeling the way I did. All the frustration, despair, anger, and confusion of the last few months had been ignited by Cecilia Martin's tragic and grotesque demise. Hearing my mother's agony had sent me over the edge. I drove around in the lunchtime traffic, cursing as I had never done before. It was as though I was possessed by profanity itself. I shouted curse words in my car, at every intersection imagining the instant destruction of Cecilia Martin and the horror of her family.

I remembered that she had sent us a sweet sympathy card after we lost BJ. She wrote, "Brad and Nina, I'm so sorry for your loss. It is so sad. But now your little one is an angel, and he is looking down on you, waiting to be with you again. God will heal your pain one day, you'll see. Fondly, Cecilia."

As I thought about how kind she was and what a violent end she met, I seethed. As I was driving by a shopping center, a car pulled out in front of me. I slammed on my breaks, stopping just short of it. Fortunately I did not have a gun in my car, or I would have shot the driver. I was completely out of control.

I stepped on the gas to catch up with the car, which had stopped ahead at a red light. In the car were three middle-aged men wearing white shirts and ties, evidently taking a break from work to get some lunch. The driver, oblivious to what he had done, was talking on a car phone.

I lost it. I went berserk. Adrenaline surged through my body. Blood rushed to my head.

Pulling my car up next to theirs, I honked my horn repeatedly. I then got out of my car and slammed my door shut. I turned to face the three men, who were now looking at me, wide-eyed with surprise.

"What is the matter with you, you idiot! Why are you such a complete idiot?" I bellowed at the driver, waving my hands violently.

The three men were clearly frightened, probably thinking I was about to shoot them. I stepped to the front of their car as the traffic light turned green. Pounding on the hood of their car, I screamed, "If you want to talk on the telephone stay in your house, you fool!"

Then, as cars started slowly passing us, drivers gawking and honking their horns, I became aware that I was standing in the middle of the street, creating a long backup of cars behind me. I walked back to my own car and quickly got in. As I was doing so, the terrified businessmen sped away, straight ahead. I saw the driver still had the phone up to his ear. Fearing he was calling the police, I too sped away, making a right turn at the intersection.

After a few moments I calmed down and realized what a ridiculous and dangerous thing I had done. But I felt strangely relaxed now. Standing in the middle of the street, stopping traffic, and maniacally shouting as loud as I possibly could had proved cathartic. But I was regretful, and surprised and frightened by my lack of self-control. I drove around a bit more, going by the corner where Cecilia had been killed two nights before. I paused as I passed the scene. Spent flares, chalk, and other debris littered the street. A large sign reading "We love you, Cecilia!" had been placed near the crosswalk.

When I arrived home, I pulled my car into the garage and just sat there in it, the engine idling. I was staring straight ahead, not really thinking of anything, but aware of my depression. I reached down for the garage door remote control to close the door, but just before I pressed the button, I realized I had not yet turned the car off. I paused for a moment, knowing that sometimes people committed suicide this way, by just breathing carbon monoxide fumes in a closed garage.

Suicide had not crossed my mind very often. When it had, I dismissed the thought as a cowardly abandoning of Nina to suffer the pangs of grief alone, or as the ultimate concession to death, the consummate confession of my defeat.

But this time I didn't seriously deliberate about the matter. I just pressed the button and the garage door began to close. I watched in my rearview mirror as the door slowly came down, pushing back the daylight with every inch it dropped. Finally as the door fell shut, the darkness leapt upon me, covering me. I sat in the pitch-black garage, with my car engine running. I still had my seatbelt on, and my hands lay motionless in my lap. I knew that if I sat there long enough, I would die. Would I then see BJ? Would my torture of sadness abate? The more I thought about it, the more attractive the idea became. As the seconds passed, I breathed deeply, trying to tell whether I felt different or if the air was bad.

After what felt like about two minutes, I began to get nervous as I thought about the possibility of dying. I feared the judgment of God. My heart beat faster, sweat gathered on my forehead, and I noticed moisture on my palms. *I could kill myself,* I thought. What would they say at my funeral? Would they bury me next to BJ? I then closed my eyes, squeezing them hard, trying to imagine the mysterious passage through death. I knew the Lord would not be pleased if I died this way. As I thought about that, I realized my hand was on the ignition key. Reflexively I jerked it toward me, turning off the engine.

I knew I needed help right away. This was self-destructive behavior. I quickly went inside and called Pastor Ed at his house, where he usually was during the day. After several rings his answering machine answered, and I said, sounding disturbed, "Hi, Ed, it's Brad, I—"

"Hi Brad, Ed here," he said, breathless. "I just walked in. What's up?"

"Ed, are you busy right now? I think I want to talk to you."

"No, I'm not really busy right now. That would be fine."

We made arrangements to meet at a large park midway between our houses. We walked around the perimeter of the park together, talking for more than an hour. He just nodded as I did most of the talking.

"Ed," I said after spending a long time describing fights with Nina and sundry episodes of depression, "I'm not getting any better. I go to the cemetery every day. I feel like I if I don't, it's disrespectful to BJ, like I've forgotten about him or denied him. But it's exhausting me. I've gained a lot of weight, I don't sleep very well, I can't concentrate on anything, I get angry for no good reason, and I'm still angry at God. I'm a mess."

"You haven't let go," he said matter-of-factly.

I looked at him.

"You haven't let go of your son, Brad," he said, stopping and facing me squarely. "You're not going to start feeling any better until you do that. You'll have to give him to God and let go of him."

His words rang true to me. I knew he was right.

"Well, Ed, I know you're right, but—"

"No," Ed said in a sure voice. "There are no buts or excuses to be made. You have to let go of your boy, give him to God, and move on as best you can. He's gone now and you have a life to live. You have to pursue healing, Brad, it won't just fall into your lap. I mean, there is still meaning and purpose to your life, and to Nina's life, and you two have a responsibility to realize that and begin seeking to live fully again. What happened to you is done, you can't change it. But you can control how you respond to it, you can choose to trust God and act in a manner that reflects your reliance upon his grace. You are the one who decides how this tragedy plays out. You are the one who tells the story of the rest of your life, and you do it with the behavioral choices you make."

We resumed walking in silence. What he said made sense to me, but it seemed difficult, and the practical means of doing it were a mystery.

"Listen," Ed said finally, "first of all, only go to the cemetery once a week, not every day. There's nothing wrong with going once each week, even less if you like. In fact, it would be better for you. You should also exercise more and get out of the house and be with friends. But the fundamental issue here, Brad, is that you have to give your baby to God. You know, listening to you talk for about an hour, I never heard you once say that you know God loves you. That needs to be a part of your understanding. You should think about that more. Instead of blaming God for what you don't have, you should thank him for what you do have. If you think about it, you'll realize that you really do have a lot to be thankful for. Gratitude, not remorse, should come to be the defining sentiment of your life. I know that is easier said than done, and you must not try to suppress your feelings of sorrow and grief, but as God's child and someone who has been the undeserved recipient of his grace, gratitude, whatever your circumstance, is warranted."

Ed continued, "God is not unaware of your pain. C. S. Lewis said that God whispers to us in our happiness but shouts to us in our pain. Maybe you've been too inwardly focused to hear God. Maybe you need to dwell less on your pain, on your feelings, on what you want and how you've been disappointed, and begin to direct some of your attention away from yourself, toward the pains and needs of others."

Stopping and turning to me again, he said, "There's kind of a paradox about grief: The more you concentrate on your own loss and your own feelings, the worse you feel, but the more you focus on God's goodness to you, and how you can serve others and help them with their despair, the clearer you understand your own pain and the faster you assimilate it. I don't mean it goes away; I mean you learn to live with it. You mature through it rather than drown in it.

"Did you ever hear the story of the poor man who had a house and a small mill and lost it all in a torrential rainstorm? Everything he had, all his possessions, everything that defined him and gave his life purpose was carried away in the flood. Standing there and surveying the damage, the devastated man wondered what he would do with himself and his shattered future. He figured his life was over. After the floodwaters had subsided, he gazed at the riverbanks the storm had scoured, and he noticed something gleaming in the faint sunlight. He made his way over to the object, and do you know what it was? It was a giant hunk of gold. The man would now be able to buy a new house and mill much nicer than the one he had lost. The tragedy that had so devastated the man and so utterly impoverished him had revealed something priceless to him that he otherwise would never have found. The storm that at first made him so poor had ultimately made him rich."

Ed went on, "Brad, you don't know the future. You don't know what God will do with you in the years to come. Don't form permanent opinions and attitudes based on present discouraging circumstances, because those views will endure into the future and may not be well-suited to the next set of circumstances you find yourself in. I know grief is all around you now, but you should not forget to look for treasures hidden in your new reality. No matter what situations God places us in, he always provides us with what we need. Always. His grace is sufficient for us. Think about that."

Our walk had brought us to an aging wooden picnic table, beneath a shade-giving oak tree. We sat down across from one another. Ed took his glasses off and slowly rubbed his eyes.

"You lost a future," he said as he put his glasses back on and looked intently at me. "That's what loss is, the deprivation of a relationship or opportunities in your days to come. But God will provide you with a new future; he will present you with other relationships and redemptive ways of living you cannot yet imagine. The scenery of your life will change, but it can still be a beautiful picture. After all, it continues to be in the hands of the same Designer."

Ed leaned toward me and raised his voice a bit. "God has not been caught by surprise at what happened to you, Brad. He is well able and eager to bring you through this. Think of Job, Abraham, Joseph, David, and Israel itself. God has an impressive record of raising people up and out of despair and desperation and teaching them some important lessons in the process. Take the devotion you are giving to grief these days, Brad, and begin to give it to God. Open yourself up to him, and what he might want you to learn from your experience. Devote yourself to trying to understand him on his terms, and you'll start to move toward healing. Now, I don't mean you'll stop feeling grief and pain, nor should you. I mean you'll start to live more fully and healthily—and maybe even more wisely—amid grief and pain."

Ed's words, though challenging, had a soothing effect. They were hard for me to take in many ways, but I knew he was trying to help me, and I knew that I had been submerged in self-absorption and self-pity. I had never once, in all the days since BJ's birth, thanked God for the good things in my life. I hadn't even thanked God that we had BJ for as long as we did, or for the joy and closeness BJ brought to our lives.

Back at the parking lot, Ed reached into the backseat of his car and picked up three books.

"Here," he said, handing them to me, "I've been waiting to give these to you. Read them when you can. Each one has something special to say."

I stood there and looked at the titles: *I'll Hold You in Heaven* by Jack Hayford; *When a Baby Dies* by Rana Limbo and Sara Rich Wheeler; and *The Tenth Good Thing About Barney* by Judith Viorst.

"Is this Barney the dinosaur?" I asked, wondering why he was giving me the book.

"No." Ed chuckled. "It's a book to help children understand the loss of a pet, but I thought it might also have something to say to you."

"Who's Barney, and what's the tenth good thing about him?" I said, getting into my car.

Ed leaned into my open window. "He was a cat."

"A cat?"

"In the story, the little boy who loses his beloved cat holds a funeral for him and buries him in his backyard. At the funeral, the boy can think of only nine good things to say about the cat. But later, while working with his father in the garden, he realizes the tenth good thing about Barney."

"What is it?"

"He will help things grow."

CHAPTER 13

Learning to Live with Loss

*C*hristmas that year was bleak. We were at Nina's parents' house surrounded by her nieces and nephews, including her sister's brand new baby, who was born about a month and a half after we lost BJ. I felt alien and misplaced, uncomfortable amidst so many kids and parents. Nina smiled and acted quite normal that day, but I could see behind her brave facade. Her hollow eyes and occasional stares into space betrayed her inward sadness. Still, she drew strength from her family, and she bore the appearance of someone resolved to live on.

We tried that December to get Nina pregnant, but failed. It was especially painful when she took the pregnancy test that month. We both expected for some reason that it would be positive, that God would grant us this deepest wish, but the straight negative line slashed those hopes immediately.

Nonetheless, the first half of 1992 saw us learn to live with the grief which had become our unwanted houseguest. Somehow we were getting along day by day. We had both learned to function, more or less, with the stress and pain of our sorrow. No secret password or breakthrough idea enabled us to do this, just the daily exercise of living. Outwardly we looked the same—except I had gained a lot of weight—but inside we were different people, changed and changing. Sorrow and sadness had battered and buffeted us, and, like a force of nature, altered our inner faces.

We were gripped by a pervasive sense of ambiguity, aware that all our plans for our lives could never be more than provisional. We did not control our futures or destinies; we could not navigate our lives to the shore of our choosing. Ambiguity was now a close partner in our lives, and, though unwelcomed at first, I realized it had a valuable role to serve: it constantly reminded us to trust God, to look to him for our comfort, sustenance, and security, and to remember our lives were in his hands. It also taught us that our true home was with him. "Hold this life loosely," Pastor Ed was fond of saying. I knew now in a clearer way than I had before that that was sound advice; to clutch at that which is temporary, transient, and beyond our control, is to insure instability and disappointment. Instead, I understood, we should cling to the goodness of God and the knowledge of his unflagging love.

Yes, God was sovereign over our lives, and his will prevailed over our best-laid plans. As we absorbed the knowledge of this ultimate dependence, we moved, however imperceptibly, toward incorporating what had happened to us into our selves, quietly accepting our new identity.

But, to our surprise, we also realized that some of the changes taking place inside of us were good. We thought more carefully about life, we sensed in a clearer way its value, and we were more sensitive to the pain and turmoil of others. Our acquaintance with deep sorrow had sensitized us to the sufferings of other people. Our ability to be compassionate grew. When we would see on the news that some child had been killed in an accident or murdered, Nina and I would send a sympathy card to the grieving family; or we would pray together for people we had heard of in the news who had been victimized in some horrible way. Certainly these were not earthshaking acts of humanitarianism on our part, but they were things we never would have done before. It never would have crossed our minds. The deaths of strangers and the sufferings of their families had new meaning to us. Our souls had grown, and we could now perceive the agonies felt by other people, whereas before our unwanted encounter with personal devastation, we would not have been capable of such empathy. Our souls, which had been sites of such complete, scorching devastation, were now beginning to sprout new buds of life. The emotional ground of our lives, which had been plowed under by sorrow, was now starting to be fertile again, and to an extent that far surpassed its previous capacity. Our loss and grief had humanized us, had connected us to the rhythms and textures of human experience in a new and more intense way. We felt more and were, in that sense, more alive.

Once, while driving somewhere together, we noticed in the car next to us a father angrily yelling at his wife and two young children. His red face and violent hand-waving, along with the frightened faces around him, made for a most unpleasant scene. Nina and I groaned at the sight, wishing we could remind him of the good in his life. On another occasion we attended a school band concert in which one of Nina's nephews participated. We smiled inwardly at the sight of stable parents with children, finding in it a simple pleasure.

As the weeks wore on, amid our sustained grief for BJ, our desire for another child remained. Each month we tried to get pregnant and each month we failed. Having another child had become our paramount hope; thus each failed attempt to conceive was a stinging rebuke. Unexpectedly we began to experience the pain of infertility. Nina had been pregnant before, so we knew it was possible, yet it remained elusive. As the light of spring dawned with its sanguine sights and sounds, we could not shake the overwhelming sense of discontent we felt. We were living between the now and the not yet. We had lost a baby, and we were in grief. At the same time we had an unforced, natural, God-given desire to try to have other children. And yet Nina was not getting pregnant, and we were increasingly aware of the fact that we did not control when or if she ever would.

We experienced a continuous, gnawing frustration at our inability to conceive. I never knew there were so many babies in the world. Nina and I began to see them everywhere. One day in May, while we walked around a mall, we counted fifteen of them in thirty minutes. I realized how fortunate we had been. Nina had no trouble getting pregnant with BJ, and yet so many couples grieve with the pain of infertility, an inward, silent agony that is utterly inscrutable to all but those who endure it. I breathed a prayer of thanksgiving to God for the ease with which we conceived BJ. Indeed we had been blessed by God in ways we had not even stopped to consider. In what other areas of our lives had we experienced God's favor and grace, and not even been aware of it?

As Nina and I drove home from the mall that day, a heavy silence surrounding us, she turned and said to me in a clear voice, "Brad, what if I never become pregnant again? What if we never do have another baby?"

I kept my gaze forward, the horror of the thought paralyzing me. After a long period of silence, I said, "Then we'll thank God that we had BJ as long as we did."

Nina said nothing, but she reached out and took my hand.

As time wore on, and the green hopefulness of spring turned into the arid realities of summer, Nina and I each came to understand in a plain but powerful way that BJ was gone. It was a sad but persistent knowledge that settled more and more into our consciousness each day, like dust slowly drifting down to earth after a powerful explosion. His passing had become a part of the furniture of our minds. Shock had completely worn away, and now we lived in the continuing awareness of what had happened to us. We were not parents, but we had been. We would not care for a newborn, though we had planned to. We did not have a baby, but we had gone through the gauntlet of obstetrical appointments, insurance forms, Lamaze classes, hospital paperwork, and, finally, labor and delivery. Our arms were empty and our hearts were heavy, but we had once held our precious child and known the soaring joy babies bring.

Amid all our feelings, we maintained the cherished hope of having another child someday, but we frankly acknowledged the possibility that our desire might never be fulfilled.

CHAPTER 14

A New Beginning

Later that May, mired in desperation to conceive again, Nina and I went back to Dr. Lloyd. We were utterly bewildered at our difficulty becoming pregnant. We somehow felt entitled to another baby, as though what we were going through indebted God to us.

When we arrived at Dr. Lloyd's office late on a Friday afternoon, the place seemed much different. It was quieter than before and mostly empty, except for a receptionist we did not recognize, typing away on a computer. We signed in and sat down together. In front of us on a magazine table was what looked like a large photo album. Nina and I silently stared at it, warily, as though it were a dangerous object. We knew what it must be.

After a moment I leaned forward and lifted it toward me, letting it drop on my lap. I opened it to the first page and saw several pictures of parents holding their newborns, often with a copy of a birth announcement under the photo. These were babies Dr. Lloyd had delivered. Nina shifted in her seat and sighed anxiously as she looked over at the pictures with a feigned indifference. I leafed quickly through the book, noticing the jubilant parents and sometimes grandparents. It hurt to see them, but we continued looking at each picture, not resisting the strange combination of sadness and hope we felt.

"Hey, you two," Dr. Lloyd suddenly called out to us, smiling, standing in the doorway leading back to the exam rooms. He looked the same as he had much earlier, tanned and well-dressed, not a hair out of place.

We exchanged pleasantries and went back with him into his office, where we had first gone after the ultrasound that horrible day. The room was the same as before, and as I entered the scene I felt an anxiety and tightness grip me, as though I were returning to the site of a catastrophic accident.

We told him of our frustration and pain at month after month failing to conceive. It was cathartic to share these feelings with someone, and he proved a patient listener.

"Okay," he said after we finished, clapping his hands together as though he had a plan. "I'd like to start Nina on Clomid, a drug to stimulate her ovulation. I think it should move things along. We give that stuff out like candy around here."

We left with the prescription that day, feeling good for having gone to see him. It made us feel as though we were being proactive, doing what we could to hasten another pregnancy. But of course we knew, as never before, the times and the seasons of our lives were not in our hands.

The Clomid proved unsuccessful, though, and late in the summer, we were back at Dr. Lloyd's, still confounded. I had called him on the phone, telling him of our lack of success, and he suggested we come in one morning for what he called a "coital test." We were to have intercourse early in the morning, then head directly to his office. Despite my apprehension at the medicalization of our intimacy, Nina and I went through with it and showed up at his office, feeling a little sheepish.

"How did it go?" Dr. Lloyd said to me with a hint of a smirk, as he briskly walked into the exam room where we were waiting.

"Not too bad, I suppose," I said, to awkward chuckles all around.

Dr. Lloyd then took a Q-tip and carefully swabbed a fluid sample from Nina.

"I want to look at this under a microscope," he said, as he transferred the sample to a viewing plate and left the room.

Nina and I sat there, wondering what he was looking for, when he popped his head in the room. "Come here, Brad, I want to show you something."

He walked me down the hall to a room with a microscope on a counter. "Look through this." He gestured to the eyepiece.

I stepped up to the microscope.

"Do you see that," he said as I peered at the slide. "Do you see the sperm, the little black dots? They're not really moving very much, are they?"

"No, I guess not," I said, not really noticing.

"Interesting," he remarked to himself, as he cleaned off the slide. "What's happened, I think, is that the Clomid has thickened Nina's cervical mucus, making it difficult for the sperm to swim. It's a motility problem. No more Clomid for her."

"You mean the Clomid has been making it harder for Nina to get pregnant?" I said, marveling at the irony.

"Well, yes," Dr. Lloyd said, a little embarrassed. We walked back to the exam room where Nina was waiting. "That's not common, but it can happen. Sorry about that."

"Yeah, well . . ." I was about to complain to him again, when Dr. Lloyd, no doubt wanting to move on to his next patients, quickly explained to Nina what was happening and sent us on our way, telling us to try some more without the Clomid.

So we left that day feeling as though we had made no progress for our efforts. Even that which was intended to help had instead hindered us.

As that summer wore on, I felt a powerful sense of helplessness. Nina and I marked the one-year anniversary of BJ's birth quietly at home, looking at the few pictures we had of him, feeling again the piercing pain of yearning.

As the fall arrived and we became busy again, I continued reflecting on our predicament. After a while I came to see that "helplessness" was the wrong way to understand our situation. Rather, I realized, we should see ourselves as dependent on God's grace, for indeed, we weren't helpless, but at rest in the easy yoke and light burden of Christ himself. We did not have to bear the weight of our destiny and manage all the forces affecting our lives—as though it were possible—but we could instead devote our energy to simply living with the One who intimately knew the nature of our suffering and had a wise and fatherly devotion to us well beyond our comprehension.

As I dwelled on this reality, occasionally reminding Nina and myself of it, I felt we had begun learning a certain patience, a sustained reliance on the compassionate hand that was always upon us.

So it was that then, when we least expected it and when our attentions were focused elsewhere, Nina took a home pregnancy test and it was positive. I was not home when she took the test, but I've often imagined how the sounds of her tears must have filled our still and silent rooms, heralding the advent of new life and declaring the sweet satisfaction of a heart's deepest longing.

When I walked in the door late that afternoon, she met me in the kitchen. Her face was red and puffy, with an almost forlorn expression. I was alarmed. She held up the test, with its bright red plus sign, but before I could react she buried her head in my chest and sobbed. They were deep cries, no doubt filled with relief and elation, but overwhelmed by the reminder of the stunning loss in which our last pregnancy had culminated. It was indeed a reflection of the depth of her grief for her lost son that even at this news she was saturated with sorrow for him.

My own reaction was more subdued than I had expected. I murmured quietly as I hugged her, feeling an immense and indescribable relief mixed with empathy for Nina's loss. We stood there together for some time, and I basked in this deliverance, whispering "Thank you" over and over. After a time we went to the couch and collapsed, dazed, but beginning to fill with delight. The meaning and magnitude of this event was dawning on us.

And yet, over the next several days, though our jubilation gradually grew, it was restrained, first, by a sense of caution, knowing from experience that it was possible we could lose our baby, and second, from a vague sense of guilt, as though to celebrate would be disrespectful to BJ or cheapen his memory. Of course that would not have actually been the case, but we both seemed reluctant to allow our feelings for him to be completely pushed aside by this unexpected though long-awaited news.

But as we shared with our family and friends our blessing, the gravity of the gift came into focus. The joyous yet often tearful reactions helped convey to us the reality of what we were experiencing, just as, about a year earlier, the grave sobriety of people told us of the profundity of our loss in a way words could not.

Nina and I now felt as though we were embarking on a long trip, one we had been on before but were not quite allowed to finish. Much of the terrain would be familiar to us, but it would not be a friendly familiarity; instead it would be an uneasy one, to be greeted with vigilance. But, as before, vigilance to me was mania to her, and our days were sometimes marked by the little battles over whether she was sufficiently "careful" working in the house, working in the yard, working at her school, whatever. Despite these brief disputes, a certain maturity had come to rest upon us. We had grown during our year of living in the house of mourning, and we saw that our lives and the life of our child were all held together in the wise, sovereign grip of our Father.

During the early weeks of this pregnancy, up to the end of her third month, Nina's hormone levels were monitored by Dr. Lloyd. He said she would need a certain level of hormones to sustain this pregnancy, and in the hopes of minimizing the chances of a miscarriage, he wanted to give her regular blood tests. This was a great psychological help to us, since, again, it made us feel as though we were being proactive, "managing" the pregnancy to the greatest extent we could. So Nina and I would go weekly to his office for the blood tests, glad to do it, but not really expecting any bad news.

Late one afternoon, in her fifth week of pregnancy, Nina and I were at home relaxing when the phone rang.

"Hello," I said, expecting it to be one of Nina's sisters, who called daily.

"Brad, it's Dr. Lloyd."

My heart fell to my feet. He sounded subdued, almost morose. I locked eyes with Nina, who was sitting nearby. My expression must have betrayed concern, because she sat straight up.

"Listen," Dr. Lloyd said, "Nina's blood work shows a hormone level that's dangerously low, and I want to try to bring it up."

I began to feel dizzy and light-headed. I ran my hand through my hair and exhaled. Nina stood up.

"I'm going to phone in a prescription for some vaginal suppositories, and I want Nina to take them. This should help. Can you get to the pharmacy near my office by 6:00 when they close?"

It was 5:30 and we would have to rush to make it. My mind started to flood with questions for Dr. Lloyd, but they would have to wait.

"I'm leaving now, Dr. Lloyd," I blurted, hanging up the phone and grabbing my keys.

"What is it, what is it?" Nina shouted, hands outstretched, pleading for an answer.

"He says your hormone level is low, and you need some suppositories. I've got to hurry."

"I'm going with you," she said.

As we sped to the pharmacy, Nina was inconsolable.

"Why is this happening? Why is this happening?" she yelled repeatedly, pulling on her hair. She started rocking back and forth holding her abdomen, much as she did on the way home from Dr. Lloyd's just after we had found out about BJ.

I tried to concentrate on the road as I contemplated our worst fears. I shared Nina's dismay, as though this should not be happening to us. Weren't we entitled to a perfect pregnancy, a problem-free passage to parenthood?

We arrived in time and picked up the pills, the elderly pharmacist giving us a warm "Good luck" as we left.

The next week Dr. Lloyd called again. Nina's levels were still low, and this time he wanted me to give her hormone shots, one a day. We went to his office for the first one, he showed me how to do it, and thereafter, for about six weeks,

I gave her the shots at home. Nina dreaded them. They were painful, and her hip started to look like a dot-to-dot puzzle, the needle marks leaving a trail of scabs. Dr. Lloyd said the chance of a miscarriage was highest during the first twelve weeks, and he wanted me to give her the shots until then.

This was a time, for us, of incredible tension. We didn't talk much of her pregnancy, the baby, or the future. But obviously miscarriage was the misery whose name we did not speak. We went about our affairs, praying, hoping, and wondering. Each night we prayed together for our baby, and the babies of other people we knew who were pregnant, asking that they would all be born "without problem or complication."

I spent a lot of my free time driving around aimlessly, contemplating the past, present, and future. One Saturday afternoon, when I was particularly anguished, I went to the cemetery. I was deeply unsettled, trying to trust in the Lord of life, but full of the fear of losing our baby and what that might do to Nina and me. I stood over BJ's tablet, staring at its inscription, remembering the day we buried him. It was a blustery fall day, and the warm breeze soothed my face.

After a while, I walked around the cemetery a bit, looking at the now familiar monuments. Off in the distance, I saw a small crowd breaking up, apparently just concluding a graveside service. They were in an adjoining cemetery, and the two separate properties made for one vast burial ground. As I studied this gathering, I realized I recognized the location. I had been there a few years earlier, visiting the grave of the Christian writer and Nazi death-camp survivor Corrie ten Boom. I had read her book *The Hiding Place*, which told her story of sheltering Jews from the Nazis, her harrowing imprisonment at Ravensbrück, and her ultimate triumph over it all, forgiving her persecutors who took so much from her, including the lives of her father, sister, brother, and nephew.

Walking toward her grave, I remembered her story and how she often said that when God tells us to love our enemies he gives, along with that responsibility, the love itself. I had once heard her on the radio. In her thick Dutch accent, she said, "It comes from him, the love comes from him."

I reached the area of her grave and wandered around looking for it. Just as I was about to give up, I found it. I had forgotten how plain it was. It read:

Corrie ten Boom
1892–1983
Jesus Is Victor

I gazed at the words, considering their message. "Jesus Is Victor" could mean so many things—in fact, it meant everything. In her own life, her suffering had been redeemed by her Savior, so that it came to have a purpose that pointed beyond itself. All the pain, injustice, hatred, and death that had touched her was vanquished by the cross. Jesus was victor, finally, over death itself, but also over every disappointment, hardship, loss, and threat we ever face. Our lives, and the pain within them, are set within the larger story of his healing love for us and its persistence. Just as he physically and emotionally felt our common suffering when he walked the earth, so he continues to stand with us, knowing our heartache, imparting his peace, and leading us on toward the eventual fulfillment—both here and beyond—of his good purpose in us. So even in sorrow and despair, we have the resolution of our deepest angst.

Indeed, I thought a lot during those weeks about God, as Pastor Ed had urged me to months earlier. I reflected on some of the attributes the Bible ascribes to him: all-loving, all-powerful, all-knowing. I found comfort and strength in these thoughts.

If God is personal and infinite, omniscient and unbounded by time, he must have known what was going to happen to BJ. In his foreknowledge, God knew, before Nina and I met, indeed, before we ever were, that we would have a stillborn son. Before I lived any of my life, God knew this would happen to me, and he knew what it would do to me.

In this light, I saw that God must have been preparing me for this tragedy my entire life. Even though I didn't know it, all of my experiences, all of my relationships, all of my ideas and feelings that had been accumulating throughout my life had been equipping me to deal with this tragedy.

I understood then, however imperfectly, that the resources I needed to survive this breathtaking and disorienting sorrow and worry were within me, placed there by the providential and beneficent hand of God himself, which, though often unrecognized by me, had always been working in my life. God's deep love and compassionate mercy—moved by his foreknowledge—had empowered me to live abundantly even in the midst of this grief and terror. The One who sees the sparrow fall, who counts the hairs on my head, the sand on the shore, and the stars in the sky, the ordainer of my days, the one who has placed his very Spirit within me to guide and comfort me, surely had not left me bereft of what I need to live. If I looked closely enough, I knew I would see his tender finger-prints all over the minutes of my days and the months of my years. My life had been formed by him, and he had touched all of me, just as the potter's hands caress every dimension of the pot. As God will never leave himself without witness in this world, I thought, so he would never leave himself without witness in my life. I had only to begin looking.

After those first three months of the pregnancy, Nina's hormone levels were raised, and Dr. Lloyd stopped monitoring her. The time began to pass more rapidly as we remained busy, guarding our growing excitement. We had thrilled to hear our new baby's heartbeat and proudly displayed our ultrasound pictures. We had a girl on the way, and every glance at the ultrasound pictures, every sight of Nina's round womb, every punch and kick of the baby spoke to us of who she might become and who her brother might have been, where we had been and where we might be going. We decided to name her Hannah, Hebrew for "grace." God had heard our cries for a child, just as he'd heard the cries of the first Hannah.

As Nina neared the end of her thirty-sixth week, Dr. Lloyd had us go to a radiology lab near his office for a precautionary ultrasound. He said he was having us do this as much for our peace of mind as any medical reason. But, once again, what we had thought would be routine proved otherwise. As the three of us—the technician, Nina, and I—were admiring Hannah during the exam, the technician's narration of what we were seeing on screen came to a stop. She was staring at the screen, studying what looked like a small blob.

"What are you looking at?" I said.

"Well," the middle-aged woman said, after an unnaturally long silence, "I don't know. I think it's a cyst on the umbilical cord, near the placenta."

I groaned. Nina said, "What?" in an incredulous voice and tried to sit up to see the screen.

I started peppering the technician with questions, but she said she had neither the knowledge or authority to answer them for us. She called Dr. Lloyd's office as Nina and I waited in the exam room, pacing like a pair of caged animals, trying to keep at bay the scenarios of disaster that had never been far from our minds.

"This is another hurdle," I said to Nina, trying to reassure us both. "This is just another challenge for us to confront."

The technician was quietly conferring with Dr. Lloyd on the phone. We watched her expressionless face.

"Here," she said, thrusting the receiver toward me. "He wants to talk to you."

"Dr. Lloyd?"

"Brad, this sounds like some kind of cyst. I don't think this is going to be a problem, but since Nina's almost at thirty-seven weeks, I want you two back to the radiology lab tomorrow. I want to do an amniocentesis, see if the baby's lungs are mature enough for delivery, and if they are, we'll induce Nina the next day. Okay?"

I agreed, told Nina the plan, and home we went, feeling both relieved and overwhelmed. The end was now in sight; we might hold Hannah in two days. Yet the ambiguous and contingent situation surrounding us was mind-boggling. Strangely though, that night we both rested well and were mostly untouched by anxiety. We were existentially exhausted, and in an ironic way this brought calm.

That night I read in Daniel the story of Shadrach, Meshach, and Abednego, the three Hebrews who refused to worship King Nebuchadnezzar's golden idol. For their refusal they were sentenced to be thrown into the fiery furnace. They told the king they would still not worship the gold, and that God would deliver them from the fiery furnace. They went on to say that even if God did not rescue them, they still would not bow down.

I was moved by their trust in God, even in the face of extreme danger and suffering. They knew their final outcome was for God to determine, not man or fate. Even if their hopes were dashed, they would still trust in the One they knew, not themselves, and not the idols of man's making. They prepared to enter the fiery furnace of human suffering, and there they were met by Christ himself.

In the stillness of that night, as Nina slept upstairs, I knew we were not alone, nor had we ever been.

The next day we were back at the radiology lab awaiting the amniocentesis. After a short while the radiologist arrived. She was a young, bookish-looking woman who kept looking at her watch. Evidently Dr. Lloyd was late in arriving, and she was not pleased with him. As she paced around the room, I sat with Nina, holding both of her hands. Nina was nervous and very much afraid of the pain this procedure would cause her. Dr. Lloyd had told us in his office that it would "hurt moderately," whatever that meant. Nina thought it meant it would hurt a lot.

After ten minutes Dr. Lloyd arrived and was greeted by an irritated look from the radiologist. He was out of breath, as though he had jogged to the room.

"Are we ready?" he said, washing his hands and slipping on some latex gloves. The ultrasound technician found Hannah. She looked so peaceful there in the womb, unaware that her world was about to be invaded.

"What if the needle hits the baby?" I asked Dr. Lloyd.

"Well, the baby will move away from it. What would you do if a needle pricked you?"

I stood there looking at Nina to see if she had any questions, but she only closed her eyes.

I was glad she did, because Dr. Lloyd, who had his back turned to her, had now turned around and was facing her, and he was holding an enormous needle. I have never seen a needle so long. He put some anesthetic on Nina's abdomen as I leaned over her face so she couldn't see the needle. Dr. Lloyd and the radiologist huddled near the ultrasound screen for a moment, deciding where the needle should enter Nina's womb. After a few seconds, Dr. Lloyd stepped over to Nina, and, leaning over her midsection, swiftly plunged the giant needle into her rounded belly. She inhaled sharply, then let out a stifled but intense moan of pain. "Ohh!"

After about two or three seconds, Dr. Lloyd withdrew the needle full of fluid from the womb.

"Okay, you did it, Nina," he said triumphantly. "I'm going to call you tonight with the results of this test. If the lungs are ready, I want to induce you tomorrow, okay? We're going to get your little girl out of there."

On the way home, Nina said the entry of that needle into her stomach was the most painful sensation she had ever felt.

As we were sitting on the couch at home resting, with Nina occasionally whimpering, the phone rang. I leapt up to get it.

"Brad, Dr. Lloyd. You're set. The test came back good. I want to induce Nina tomorrow. Are you ready for that?"

"Oh yeah, we're ready. You better believe it."

"Okay, then, show up at the hospital bright and early at 6:00 a.m., and we'll get it done."

We called our family to tell everyone about the next day, and, when 6:00 a.m. came, we were there at the hospital. As we were settling into our room, just down the hall from where we had BJ, we heard a soft knock on the door. In walked MaryAnn, our nurse when we had BJ.

"Oh, Nina!" she said walking over to Nina and hugging her. "I knew you'd be back here, I just knew it!"

She sat and talked for a while, saying how much she had thought of us the last year and a half. After about two hours, Dr. Lloyd arrived.

"The big day is here!" he announced as he walked in, smiling broadly. "Are you feeling well?" he asked Nina, sitting next to her on the bed.

He checked her stomach, felt her cervix, and said, "I'm going to break your water to get things moving."

Nina's labor moved quickly, as MaryAnn came in every half hour to check on her. Nina had an epidural for pain relief around noon, and at 1:30 MaryAnn examined her again.

"Wow," she said, surprised, "you've moved a lot. You feel like you're almost eight centimeters dilated to me. We've got to get Dr. Lloyd in here and get you pushing."

Nina and I exchanged a look of intense anticipation as MaryAnn started bustling around the room. Dr. Lloyd came in and without saying anything started washing his hands.

"Okay, Nina," he said, still scrubbing, "we're going to have you push hard. Try to follow my directions as best you can."

As he slipped his gloves on, MaryAnn was hurrying around the room, getting it ready for the delivery. She slid a big tray with instruments over next to Nina, brought the light down from the ceiling, and removed the end portion of Nina's bed, where her legs were.

I felt my heart race and forehead sweat as I walked over to Nina's left side and grabbed her hand. Nina's eyes looked focused, as though she were concentrating, and her teeth seemed clenched. Dr. Lloyd sat in front of her as MaryAnn placed Nina's feet in stirrups.

"Okay," Dr. Lloyd said, "a few good strong pushes, and I think you're going to have a baby here. All right, you ready? Brad, why don't you count for us. Go ahead, Nina, start pushing now."

"One, two, three, four, five, six . . ." I announced, as Nina pressed her chin against her chest and strained.

"Come on, Nina, you can do it, go ahead and push as strong as you can," MaryAnn urged.

"Good," Dr. Lloyd said as I reached ten. "That was very good. I think you made a lot of progress on that one. A couple more of those and you are going to be there."

We repeated the process three more times, each time Nina pushing harder and harder, and grunting louder and louder.

"Okay," Dr. Lloyd said, scooting his stool closer to Nina, "this time I think the baby will crown, and we'll get to see the top of her head."

My stomach fluttered as Dr. Lloyd shouted, "Push!"

"One, two, three, four, five, six, seven, eight . . ." I counted steadily.

Nina was groaning loudly as Dr. Lloyd said, "There, Brad, look at this."

He pointed toward Nina, and there was the top of Hannah's head, clearly visible. She had brown hair.

"There she is!" I said to Nina, my excitement uncontrollable. "Push again, honey, real hard, and she'll be out!"

Dr. Lloyd attached a suction cone to Hannah's head and said again, "Push!"

Nina closed her eyes, gritted her teeth, and pulled taut her facial muscles as she let out a sustained, "Uhhh!"

"One, two, three, four, five, six . . ."

"Here she comes," Dr. Lloyd interrupted my count, his voice rising with anticipation.

I stepped down toward Dr. Lloyd, leaned in, and saw my daughter's head ease out of Nina. She was face down with her eyes closed. She was covered with fluid and blood. Dr. Lloyd said nothing, cradling Hannah's head as he suctioned her mouth and nose. I was suddenly aware of how quiet the room was, and how quiet Hannah was. She was not crying or whimpering or making any noise at all. Shouldn't she be making noise?

"Ohh," I groaned, placing my hands over my mouth, as I saw the umbilical cord wrapped once around Hannah's neck. Instinctively I stepped forward, as though I was going to get the cord off from around her, but Dr. Lloyd quickly and easily loosened it and pulled it over Hannah's head. The room was still silent as I stared intently at Hannah, willing her to cry or make some noise. As Dr. Lloyd suctioned her again, her body slid out, and her newborn voice faintly cried, "Aahh."

I sighed heavily and instantly broke into a bright smile. I turned to Nina, who was beaming at Hannah with full and complete joy.

"Hello, baby!" I said, looking at Hannah as Dr. Lloyd quickly cleaned her. "Hello, Hannah, Mommy and Daddy love you!"

She was wiggling in Dr. Lloyd's arms, squinting and flailing her tiny arms. She was a vision of absolute beauty, a strong and healthy baby.

Dr. Lloyd handed Hannah to MaryAnn, who was standing next to him. MaryAnn took Hannah in the towel she was holding, folded it around her in an instant, and quickly stepped toward Nina. With great vigor Nina thrust her arms straight out toward Hannah. Nina then took her into her arms, cradled her, and brought her tenderly to her chest.

"I love you, Hannah," Nina whispered and wept, looking deeply into Hannah's puffy little face, baptizing her with her falling tears.

After a couple thrilling days we took Hannah home and started to learn the lessons new parents learn. But we never stopped thinking about BJ and how we missed him. In time, our painful yearnings for him began gradually to change into a calm acceptance of the past. Though we continued to think about what his life with us would have been like, we did so soberly, knowing it would never be. Still, we knew that he was—and would always be—a part of our lives, a significant part of ourselves and how we related to the world. We had been his parents for nine stirring and inspiring months, but God, for his own reasons, chose to take BJ back unto himself.

It seemed now our grief for him had burned through us, and, although feelings of loss, sadness, and hurt persisted—ebbing and flowing with our moods and the other events of our daily lives—there was subtly coming over us a hint of contentedness. Of course the joy Hannah brought us helped, but she did not erase or replace BJ. No, his life had forever touched us, and absorbing the reality of losing him transformed us, as great loss always does.

In the struggle of the night, the quickest way for anyone to reach the light is not to chase the sun into the west, where it last was. Rather, one finds the rosy fingers of dawn earliest by, paradoxically, heading east, into the darkness itself.

So it often is with grief. Yearning for what we have lost, holding on to a past to which we know we can never return, leads us only further into darkness. But if we let the night come upon us, moving into grief and experiencing the dark night of the soul, we sooner—and perhaps unexpectedly—come to see the hopeful shades of dawn and the soft embrace of the morning star.

But the profound grief of great loss never totally vanishes. Amid the cycles and seasons of life and throughout the ups and downs of each day, loss and regret return, and the scar of grief occasionally throbs. Then, again, these feelings yield to the larger meaning of our lives. This is the "new normal," which defines the personality of one who has encountered and authentically experienced deep loss. The trauma of a psychological and emotional cataclysm leaves an imprint on the soul, and it is a permanent contour.

But, like all other realities, we can resolve to see it with the eyes and heart of our heavenly Father. He is the one who has always known the end from the beginning. He is the one who alone knows the answers to our deepest questions. He is the one who has graciously given us new life through his Son. And so it is, that, in a different sense, God also provided Nina and me with new life—through BJ, our beloved baby, who will always be sacred to our memory.

Resources

*H*ere is a general list of some organizations which offer support in the form of newsletters, pamphlets, books, tapes, and workshops for people who have experienced miscarriage, stillbirth, or infant loss. Upon request, each organization will supply information about their specific philosophy and services.

AMEND (Aiding a Mother Experiencing Neonatal Death)
4324 Berrywick Terrace
St. Louis, MO 63128

A Place to Remember (memory boxes, baby books,
    cards, etc.)
de Ruyter-Nelson Publications
1885 University Avenue, Suite 110
St. Paul, MN 55104

Association for Recognition of Life of Stillbirths
11128 West Front Avenue
Littleton, CO 80127

Center for Loss in Multiple Births
P. O. Box 1064
Palmer, AK 99645

Centering Corporation (grief resource center)
P. O. Box 3367
Omaha, NE 68103–0367

Compassionate Friends, Inc.
National Headquarters
P. O. Box 3696
Oak Brook, IL 60522–3696

MIDS, Inc. (Miscarriage, Infant Death, Stillbirth)
c/o Janet Tischler
16 Crescent Drive
Parsippany, NJ 07054

MISS (Mothers In Sympathy and Support)
8448 West Aster Drive
Peoria, AZ 85381

National Sudden Infant Death Syndrome Foundation
P. O. Box 3044
Oakton, VA 22124–3044

Pen-Parents, Inc. (correspondence network for
    bereaved parents)
P. O. Box 8738
Reno, NV 89507–8738

Perinatal Loss Project
2116 N. E. 18th Avenue
Portland, OR 97212–2621

Pregnancy and Infant Loss Center
1421 East Wayzata Boulevard
Wayzata, MN 55391

Resolve, Inc. (infertility)
1310 Broadway
Somerville, MA 02144–1731

Resolve Through Sharing
La Crosse Lutheran Hospital
1910 South Avenue
La Crosse, WI 54601

SHARE (A Source of Help in Airing and Resolving
    Experiences)
Pregnancy and Infant Loss Support, Inc.
St. Joseph Health Center
300 First Capitol Drive
St. Charles, MO 63301

SIDS Alliance (Sudden Infant Death Syndrome)
10500 Little Patuxent Parkway, Suite 420
Columbia, MD 21044

Annotated Bibliography

*T*his is a brief description of helpful books which address the general subjects of grief and grieving, particularly following miscarriage, stillbirth, infant, and childhood death.

Bramblett, John. *When Good-Bye Is Forever: Learning to Live Again After the Loss of a Child.* Foreword by C. Everett Koop. New York: Ballantine Books, 1991. This extraordinarily poignant book tells the story of the Bramblett family's anguish at losing their two-year-old son Christopher in an accident. From the tragedy itself, to the many months that followed, John Bramblett honestly and clearly shares his sadness as a father. This book includes comments from Mairi Bramblett, Christopher's mother, as well as from their other children, giving the reader a picture of the full impact this loss has on the whole family.

Davis, Deborah L. *Empty Cradle, Broken Heart: Surviving the Death of Your Baby.* Revised and expanded edition. Golden, Colo.: Fulcrum Publishing, 1996. The author is a psychologist who majors in perinatal bereavement, and this sensitively written book is packed with thoughts and advice from parents who have lost babies. It also contains many bibliographical and organizational references.

Habermas, Gary. *Forever Loved: A Personal Account of Grief and Resurrection.* Joplin, Mo.: College Press, 1997. Well-known Christian scholar Gary Habermas lost his wife Debbie to cancer, leaving him a single parent to four children. This book chronicles her passing and the struggle with grief that Habermas and his family endure. Among Habermas's inspiring thoughts are ruminations on God's goodness despite human suffering.

Hayford, Jack. *I'll Hold You in Heaven.* Ventura, Calif.: Regal Books, 1990. This short work offers biblical counseling from a veteran pastor and author. Pastor Hayford's easy-to-read style makes difficult issues understandable. He focuses on loss through miscarriage, stillbirth, and infant death, but also includes lengthy discussions of post-abortion grief and guilt.

Kohn, Ingrid and Perry-Lynn Moffitt with Isabelle A. Wilkins. *A Silent Sorrow—Pregnancy Loss: Guidance and Support for You and Your Family.* New York: Dell Publishing, 1992. This complete treatment of pregnancy loss includes helpful sections on the different ways men and women grieve, the feelings of grandparents, and the unique pain of infertility. The glossary and extensive bibliography are informative.

Limbo, Rana K. and Sara Rich Wheeler. *When a Baby Dies: A Handbook for Healing and Helping.* La Crosse, Wis.: Resolve Through Sharing in conjunction with La Crosse Lutheran Hospital, 1986. Compiled by two registered nurses who specialize in bereavement, this comprehensive treatment of perinatal loss and the trauma it inflicts is an indispensable resource for parents, relatives, nurses, and physicians. The thorough bibliography and practical suggestions for caregivers are outstanding. Both authors are directors of Resolve Through Sharing.

Lewis, C. S. *A Grief Observed.* New York: Bantam Books, 1976. A classic theological reflection by the well-known Christian writer, in which he shares his anger, dismay, and desolation at the loss of his wife of four years, Joy Davidman.

Mehren, Elizabeth. *After the Darkest Hour the Sun Will Shine Again: A Parent's Guide to Coping with the Loss of a Child.* Foreword by Harold S. Kushner. New York: Simon and Schuster, 1997. This fascinating book chronicles the losses of parents—famous and unknown, historical and contemporary—and offers hope and encouragement through simple, comforting thoughts. The author lost her own daughter two months after birth.

Nash, Ronald H. *When a Baby Dies: Answers to Comfort Grieving Parents.* Grand Rapids: Zondervan, 1999. This short, readable work is an examination of the theological issues surrounding infant death. Professor Nash carefully offers a biblical basis for grieving parents to trust they will see their children again.

Santorum, Karen Garver. *Letters to Gabriel: The True Story of Gabriel Michael Santorum.* Irving, Tex.: CCC of America, 1998. This is a touching collection of letters that Karen Santorum, wife of U.S. Senator Rick

Santorum, wrote to her son Gabriel each day of her pregnancy. We share the Santorums' joy with their baby, their heartbreak at finding out he has a life-threatening kidney disorder, their desperate struggle to save him, and his eventual premature birth at twenty weeks. Gabriel died two hours after birth, but the beautiful impression he made on the lives of his parents and family is forever preserved in this moving book.

Schwiebert, Pat and Paul Kirk. *When Hello Means Good-bye: A Guide for Parents Whose Child Dies Before Birth, at Birth, or Shortly After Birth.* Portland, Ore.: Perinatal Loss Project, 1985. This practical handbook for parents will also help family and friends of the bereaved partially understand what parents who have just lost their baby are experiencing. The short book presents thoughts and poems from mourning parents, as well as a wide range of urgent and useful advice, such as the need to name your baby, the value of keepsakes, ways to memorialize the birth and death of your baby, how to find a funeral home, etc. This is an extremely valuable guide that helps parents cope with the shock of stillbirth and infant loss. Pastors and counselors should keep copies on hand.

Sittser, Gerald L. *A Grace Disguised: How the Soul Grows Through Loss.* Grand Rapids: Zondervan, 1995. This genuinely profound investigation into the nature of grief is a precious companion for anyone learning to live with loss. Gerald Sittser writes with unmatched clarity about losing his mother, wife, and four-year-old daughter when their family car was struck by another vehicle being driven by a drunk driver. Of all the books on loss with which I am familiar, this is the single most instructive and redemptive volume.

Vredevelt, Pam M. *Empty Arms: Emotional Support for Those Who Have Suffered Miscarriage, Stillbirth, or Tubal Pregnancy.* Sisters, Ore.: Multnomah Books, revised edition, 1991. This sensitive meditation on grief, anger, and guilt—written by a woman who lost her baby when she was five months pregnant—is a deeply insightful and rewarding book. The author is a Licensed Professional Counselor who specializes in grief therapy.

Wolterstorff, Nicholas. *Lament for a Son.* Grand Rapids: William B. Eerdmans, 1987. This is a wise and penetrating reflection on loss and how it psychologically and spiritually affects us. Professor Wolterstorff is a leading Christian philosopher whose adult son died in a mountain-climbing accident. This book is the personal journal he kept of his experience grieving.

We want to hear from you. Please send your comments about this book to us in care of the address below. Thank you.

ZONDERVAN™

GRAND RAPIDS, MICHIGAN 49530 USA

WWW.ZONDERVAN.COM